The Reverend Stephen A. Blakey, BSc BD OStJ.

Stephen A. Blakey was born in the house where the Scottish poet Robert Burns died, and it seems that he might have inherited some character traits from Bard himself.

Blakey's love for Rugby Union may have interfered with his academic studies but in due course it provided an invaluable point of contact with his military parish. The longest serving chaplain in the British Army, with over 40-year service, he ministered to every element of what is now the Royal Regiment of Scotland…at home and overseas, in war and in peace, on the rugby park and in church.

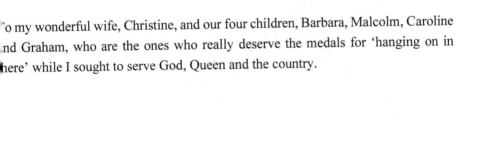

To my wonderful wife, Christine, and our four children, Barbara, Malcolm, Caroline and Graham, who are the ones who really deserve the medals for 'hanging on in here' while I sought to serve God, Queen and the country.

Stephen A. Blakey

THE PADRE WAS A HOOKER

Reflections on 40 years as an
Army Chaplain

AUSTIN MACAULEY PUBLISHERS™

LONDON • CAMBRIDGE • NEW YORK • SHARJAH

A CIP catalogue record for this title is available from the British Library.

ISBN 9781788230780 (Paperback)
ISBN 9781788230803 (Hardback)
ISBN 9781788230865 (ePub e-book)

www.austinmacauley.com

First Published (2021)
Austin Macauley Publishers Ltd
25 Canada Square
Canary Wharf
London
E14 5LQ

owe a great debt of thanks to all those with whom I have served over these past four decades. From the chaplains in the Royal Army Chaplains' Department, to the officers and soldiers of the various battalions I was honoured to minister to, and to the military community, which we were all part of. My story is their story, and I am grateful for the opportunity to put some of it down in paper and ink.

I would like to thank David Blake, curator of the Museum of Army Chaplaincy for his encouragement over many years to 'sit down and write that book you are always talking about', and for his always prompt and accurate response to requests for names, places and dates.

The staff of the Farmington Institute, Harris Manchester College, Oxford provided a wonderful opportunity for academic retreat and study which stirred my long-lost desire to read more deeply. Thank you.

And to my team at home. Christine, Evelyn Hood, Carolyn Richmond and Dr Deryck Lovegrove. Thank you for your patience, your proof reading, and your encouragement at every stage of this project. This would quite simply not exist without you. And to Andrew Richmond of Old Craig Photography, thank you!

Table of Contents

Chapter 1
In the Beginning

"The secret to getting ahead is getting started." – Mark Twain

There is a tradition in Scotland of giving a new-born child a silver coin to bring good luck. If the child receives the coin with a strong grasp, it suggests that he or she will grow up to be careful with their money. However, if the coin is dropped quickly, you've perhaps got a shopaholic on your hands.

I first became aware of this tradition when my Blakey grandfather came to visit my brother Colin on his arrival home from the maternity hospital with our mother. I have no memory of how the baby responded to the generous gift, but I do recall Grandpa saying, "Aye, he'll be a soldier when he grows up." Of all of us four brothers, Colin is the least military in all sorts of ways, but he did become an accountant, so maybe that coin had a part to play after all.

As for me, I don't think anyone would ever have guessed or prophesied that I would become a soldier, or more correctly, a soldiers' minister. I was born in the house in Dumfries in which Robert Burns had died. The nearest link my birth gave me to anything military was probably Robert Burns' membership of the local militia and the military funeral they provided when he died in poverty. I have always resisted any suggestion that I inherited any of his other character traits such as a fondness of the drink and falling out with Presbytery.

I was in my late twenties before I realised that I had been born in such a famous location. My wife, Christine, had been encouraging me to explore my roots and this prompted me to phone the local authority office in Dumfries to ask where and what was the 'Burns House, Dumfries' which was recorded as the place of birth on my Birth Certificate. "It is the last house where Robert Burns lived, and is now a museum," I was informed.

Further questions revealed that while the whole building is in fact a museum in the 1950s public access was limited to the ground floor, with the caretaker and family living upstairs. The caretaker in 1953 was a Mr Creasey, my mother's father. I was born there because my mother's husband banned her from the marital home when she became pregnant with me. My mother had five children, two (or possibly three) of whom were illegitimate. Despite her protestations, that he really was the father, my mother failed to persuade him to take me into his home and so to save her marriage she arranged for me to be fostered. After four years in a privately arranged foster family, she reluctantly put me up for adoption.

It took another four years before my adoption was successfully completed. The first attempt failed and resulted in me being put into Quarriers Homes orphanage in Bridge of Weir to await another potential family to show an interest and in due course the Blakeys decided to provide me with a home, and a long and very happy family life followed. We lived for a few years in Killermont on the north side of Glasgow, before moving to St Andrews when I was eleven years old.

By 1976, I had graduated from St Andrews University, and was now at Edinburgh University studying theology in preparation for becoming a minister in the Church of Scotland. It was during my time at New College, Edinburgh that Christine and I met and were married, and were now expecting our first child. I had decided that rather than go straight into parish ministry that I would like to try and serve some years as an army chaplain. My application was being processed, I was fairly confident that I would be accepted, and we decided that it was time to inform my parents.

"They won't take just anybody," was my father's response to my plan. Although always proud of all that his sons achieved, he was from a generation of Scottish fatherhood that preferred humility over excessive self-confidence. It was a 'don't count your chickens' piece of advice, and he certainly did not want me to assume too much.

We were gathered for the evening meal – confusingly given so many different names across the land – tea, high tea, supper, dinner. Whatever we called it; it was often a fairly chaotic half hour in the Blakey family home in St Andrews. My three brothers, who at this stage were 15, 13 and 11 years of age, had far too much energy, and too little patience, to sit and eat quietly. I was a 23-year-old theology student, married with our first child on the way, and exploring

12

whether my future career as a Church of Scotland minister might be as an army chaplain.

Christine and I had been married for just over a year, and we had come to visit and to share our most recent news, which was always a slightly tense moment, as our updates to my family in the past had included an engagement, a marriage, a pregnancy, all in quick succession, and my parents might well have wondered what was going to come next.

"So, I've applied to join the Royal Army Chaplains' Department when I graduate next year," I announced. It took everyone by surprise.

My only contact with the military as a teenager had been when we used to traipse along from Madras College, South Street building in St Andrews to the Volunteer Hall once a week for Physical Education. The hall was the home to 6 Platoon, B Company, 15 Parachute Regiment, and was a large purpose-built building on City Road in the heart of St Andrews, a hub of activity for both military and civilian social events. It had a very large drill hall which was well-suited to school PE classes. (The building was sold in 1993 and is now a group of modern apartment blocks.) Apart from doing PE in the drill hall, it would be fair to say that I really had no useful knowledge or experience of the Armed Services, though my friends and I used to cycle annually the six miles from St Andrews to RAF Leuchars so we could sneak in to enjoy the RAF Air Show.

One of my best pals growing up in St Andrews, John Darroch, had joined the Royal Navy straight from school and by the time I was reading theology he was flying helicopters and, according to himself, was enjoying a great life. John came to visit Christine and me in Edinburgh where I was starting my third and final year at New College, reading Hebrew, Language and History, as a candidate for the ministry of the Church of Scotland.

"You should join the Navy as a chaplain, Steve," John offered over a beer, "you would make a great bish." Now there was an idea! Chaplains in the Royal Navy are usually given the nickname 'bish', clearly short for bishop, and probably just to be different from the army tradition of calling chaplains 'padre'. I had never thought about military chaplaincy, but the idea did take root in my thoughts and eventually bore fruit.

I was starting to fret about becoming a parish minister and whether I was quite ready for all that I imagined this might entail. This was in 1976 and I was in my final year of academic study. If all went to the normal plan, I would complete my degree and then spend one year as a Probationer Assistant before looking for a parish of my own. It all did seem to be happening very quickly.

One of my recurring nightmares was about having to give a talk to the Women's Guild. This was not helped by the New College elocution tutor Miss Balfour-Brown from Kelvinside in Glasgow. Every student studying for the ministry of the Church of Scotland was required to train for, and pass, a public speaking examination. The previous week, at my one-to-one session with Miss B-B, she had given me a text to read. "Just stand at this lectern, Mr Blakey, and imagine that you are addressing a gathering of the Guild," she instructed in her strong distinctive West End of Glasgow voice. I have always hated role-play and this was all too much for me. I stammered my way through the session and decided never to return.

I did still have to pass my Speech Test towards the end of that term, reading in front of the whole year group in the Martin Hall of New College, and this I did successfully with my loud resonating voice, which in years to come was found to be well-suited to leading worship with the troops on the parade square.

I do sometimes wonder whether my non-attendance is recorded somewhere in the depths of a filing cabinet in New College. And whether my other non-attendances are also listed. I did struggle to balance my academic studies, with married life which would soon include our new baby, completing the requirements of training for the Church of Scotland ministry, and playing rugby. More often than not it was the academic side which lost out... or perhaps the rugby which won. In my first year I had discovered that the Ecclesiastical History lectures and course requirements were a repeat of the previous year (well, perhaps of many years!) and rather than attend afternoon lectures and miss rugby training, I bought a complete set of neatly written lecture notes from a student who had taken the course the previous year, and passed the course.

There was also the day when I put my hand up to ask a question of Dr Gray, one of our Practical Theology lecturers. He listened carefully to what I imagined was quite an erudite comment on his lecture, before replying to the class, "If Mr Blakey attended more of my lectures, we would all be saved from him asking such stupid questions." Good point, Dr Gray.

The end of my academic studies was in sight, along with the prospect of parish ministry drawing ever closer. I decided to explore John Darroch's suggestion of Naval chaplaincy and Christine and I were invited over to Rosyth to meet an RN chaplain. So began a process which I suspect in the end of the day ame down to whoever was the better salesman. The competition was between the said Naval chaplain and one particular army chaplain.

Our visit to Rosyth was not a roaring success. The Naval chaplain and his wife were charming and welcoming. They answered all our questions and enthusiastically encouraged us to prayerfully consider the Royal Navy as a career. Unfortunately, the pretty disgusting South African sherry, the off-centre and squint picture above their fireplace, and their sweet eight-year-old daughter tipping the peanuts onto my lap, combined to provide a negative counterbalance to all their genuine and well-intended efforts. And when the chaplain talked about Restricted Areas in the shipyard from which the chaplain was excluded, and the small percentage of time a chaplain might spend at sea during his first three-year appointment, I did start to wonder if this was God's plan for us.

Perhaps the army chaplaincy might be the answer? So, we responded to a suggestion from one of the secretarial staff in New College, whose cousin was married to an army padre, Rev Stewart Hynd, who at the time was chaplain to 1st Battalion, The Black Watch based in Colchester, and who had generously offered to host a visit by any theology student who would like to consider ministry in the army as a possible career choice.

Divine guidance comes in many shapes and forms, and in this case, it came through a military rail warrant for a free return journey from Edinburgh to Colchester, three days familiarisation visit with the Black Watch, and a feeling that 'I could do this, and make a good go of it!' This was reinforced by the need of the Church of Scotland to find a sufficient number of year-long placements for the large number of ministry candidates graduating in the summer of 1977. In the present situation in which trainee ministers are like hen's teeth, it is hard to imagine that there was a time when the Church of Scotland had too many probationers. Probationers were typically trainees for parish ministry who had completed their academic training and were now required to carry out a year-long attachment which would provide full-time supervised practical training in a parish setting before being ordained into their first parish post.

The Kirk decided that if the army wanted me, and I wanted the army, then I could serve my probationary period as an army chaplain. (The status of probationer is similar to that of curate in the Anglican church.) Certain restrictions were put in place to ensure that I had sufficient supervision during my first year of ordained ministry, but these were pretty flexible and readily accepted by the Royal Army Chaplains' Department. I was, for example, to work

15

under the leadership of a more senior Church of Scotland chaplain, and I was barred from being deployed on overseas operations until this year was completed.

The summer of 1977 was a pretty crazy three months. I was licenced to preach the Gospel (and so became a Reverend) by the Presbytery of St Andrews on 26 June and graduated with Honours in Old Testament in July. Christine' father was Norwegian, and the family had an amazingly beautiful holiday home or hytte, called Lillevik just outside Kristiansand, and we went there for most of July and August. I looked after our six-month old daughter Barbara while Christine worked as a physiotherapist in the local hospital in Kristiansand until the time came for us to return to Scotland and for me to be ordained as a Church of Scotland minister and commissioned into the RAChD on 30 August.

The Ordination and Commissioning Service was a very meaningful and moving event. There is something awe-inducing in kneeling on the floor while 20 or 30 black robed ministers of the Kirk gather round to lay hands on you in the moment of ordination. My other lasting memory of that evening in Martyrs Church, St Andrews, is of a group of army chaplains in service dress uniform pushing the Assistant Chaplain General's army car along North Street to bump start it. I don't know if Rev Farquhar Lyall had left his lights on, and back then one wouldn't have dared to make such a suggestion, but it was a good team effort, a good introduction to my colleagues, and a source of amusement for the rest of the congregation.

And so the journey had begun. I was the youngest minister ever commissioned as a chaplain into the British army and had joined a family of Church of Scotland chaplains who held a special place in the Kirk, with a particular relationship within the Royal Army Chaplains' Department. I would continue to serve in various forms long enough to become the longest serving British military chaplain in the history of RAChD (regular and reserve service combined).

I had received my first posting order a couple of months previously and, therefore, knew that I would start my army service in Edinburgh, and so before heading off to the south to be 'made into' an army chaplain proper, I was invited by the Commanding Officer, 1st Battalion, Royal Highland Fusiliers to drop by 'to say hello'. It might have felt as casual as it sounds to Lt Col Campbell, but to me it was a pretty terrifying experience. The battalion was based in Redford Barracks on the south side of Edinburgh: A large military complex built in the years prior to the First World War to alleviate the cramped military infantry accommodation at Edinburgh Castle and to replace the substandard cavalry troops barracks at Piershill. (See Appendix C for more details about the history of Redford Barracks.)

Having never previously been inside an army barracks, and feeling extremely nervous, I decided to park on an adjacent road and approach the main gate on foot. The fact that I for the very first time was wearing a clerical collar in a public place, away from a church building, added to my stress. The soldiers on duty at the gate had, of course, been briefed that I was due to visit. Goodness knows what they thought of the fresh-faced, nervous-looking minister who appeared exactly on time but had no idea where to go or what to do.

In the midst of all my nervousness that day, I learnt one of the changeless dynamics of military life i.e., nothing stays the same. I was meeting the commanding officer, but was informed that he would no longer be CO when I completed my Sandhurst course and officially reported for duty. To my mind, in those days of innocence, it would have made more sense for me to wait until the new CO was in place, but I would in due course learn that the 'appointment' is almost always more important and more relevant than the 'person'. Meeting the commanding officer was an important thing to do.

I survived my visit, discovered the joys of chilli sherry as a way of adding a little flavour to the soup at lunch, and spent the afternoon in the officers' mess TV room watching a test match with my predecessor Rev Beverly Gauld, who was about to leave the army at the end of a short service commission. It was an unusual handover. Bev was a family friend through my Meiklejohn cousins in Glasgow, and he clearly felt that he had some wisdom to share with me regarding the quality of various RHF personalities. His time in the military had not been totally happy. Fortunately, my ignorance of matters military and my passion for test match cricket combined, with the result that very little went in, and perhaps I was saved from bringing Bev's personal emotional baggage into my first posting.

Before that posting could begin, however, I had to go through that wonderful metamorphosis which turns a civilian into a soldier. So, it was off to Bagshot Park and the Royal Military Academy, Sandhurst, and seven weeks that would change my life.

I had been to Bagshot Park previously when I'd reported for my initial interview with the Chaplain General, Rev Peter Mallet in March 1977. After a long train journey down to London from Edinburgh, I had eventually made my way to Bagshot Railway Station. It was dark by the time the train arrived, but I followed the directions, went across the main road, through the large iron gates, and up the driveway. I now know that I was not the first potential chaplain to end up lost on the long drive, knocking on the farmhouse door and being redirected further up the drive to the big house.

I did, in due course, make my way safely to the house, and the following day was interviewed by the Chaplain General. Well, I say 'interviewed' but my memory of that half hour is that Rev Peter Mallet perched on the corner of his very large desk and spoke at me for at least twenty minutes before declaring, "Welcome to the department. You will make a great army chaplain." I'm not sure that I said all that much, but perhaps that was to my benefit.

Bagshot Park was at this time the regimental headquarters and depot of the Royal Army Chaplains' Department. The house was built as a wedding gift from Queen Victoria to her son Prince Arthur, Duke of Connaught and Strathearn. It was the home for army chaplains from shortly after the Second World War until the late 1990s when the Earl and Countess of Wessex took over the tenancy from the Crown Estates.

Many chaplains of my generation look back to Bagshot Park with fond memories. The house was run by a small team headed up by the warden, a senior army chaplain who lived in what had been the nursery wing of the house. The quality of the humour of any new warden could be discerned by whether or not he allowed the 'Please do not walk on the water' sign to remain in public view. Situated beside the very large rectangular fish pond, it looked so much like a normal 'Please do not walk on the grass' sign it was easy to miss, but amongst those who did recognise it were a few who took offence, didn't find it at all funny, and had it hidden from sight.

The original sign was removed when the chaplains left, but a new one, made by J.M.J. Holland Chair-makers and presented to the Earl of Wessex, has replaced it and is still *in situ.*

On 2 September 1977 I headed off to Bagshot Park once again. All the academic training, and the interviews and selection were over, and this time I was reporting for duty as an officer in the Royal Army Chaplains' Department. I was hugely excited and incredibly nervous. I had very little idea what to expect of the next few weeks, but it was too late to change my mind and so I put on a brave face and got on with it.

That evening at Bagshot I met up with my fellow new intake chaplains: John Whitton, Peter Howson, Alan Brown and Brian Elliot.

We would spend five weeks together and become well acquainted. We were a pretty motley crew, but I think that is often the case with clergy. As a theology student at New College, Edinburgh I had often looked around the common room at my fellow candidates for Church of Scotland ministry, and wondered what is wrong with me that I fitted in with such a mixed bag of folk? And here at Bagshot I found more of the same.

We varied in all sorts of ways: in age (from me at 24 to Alan Brown at 35), in height (Alan Brown at one end of the spectrum to Peter Howson at the other, with legs far too long for a thirty inch marching stride), in churchmanship (two Anglicans, two Church of Scotland and one Methodist) and in military experience – basically none except that John, Alan and Brian had joined a couple of months earlier and so had already spent time with their unit of attachment and took every opportunity to ensure that Peter and I were fully aware of their vast knowledge.

Despite all, we blended well and survived everything that Bagshot and the Royal Military Academy, Sandhurst could throw at as. After five days or so dealing with chaplaincy matters, filling in forms, signing the Official Secrets Act, and being issued with a bewildering variety of uniform, we were dropped off at Victory College for the CMDVLP Course. It is now called the PQO Course (Professionally Qualified Officers) which is less awkward than chaplains, medics, dentists, vets and postal and communications officers' course, but still doesn't work nearly as well as the 'Tarts and Vicars Course' by which the rest of the military academy referred to us. It is designed for those officers who, prior to being commissioned into the army, have become fully qualified in the civilian profession for which they have been recruited by the military. Our ages varied from mid-twenties to mid-forties, so we stood out amidst the bright and much younger officer cadets of the academy.

In those days this course for chaplains lasted for one month and was a distillation of the three-month first term attended by the university graduate officers' intake. The main aim of the course seemed to be survival, i.e., that we would survive our first postings without doing anything stupid, wearing the wrong uniform, being in the wrong place, getting lost, breaking any rules or bringing the army into disrepute. I really enjoyed my time at Sandhurst and according to my 'Personnel File' I passed out as the top chaplain on the course. I, of course, have never actually seen a P file, but I am led to believe that there is one for each officer, and that it contains every piece of paper and information about your career that comes across the desk of the clerks at the Ministry of Defence personnel headquarters.

Having successfully completed the course and passed off the square, the next challenge was to get home. I had travelled down from Edinburgh seven weeks previously with just one large suitcase. In the interim I had gathered an enormous amount of uniform, equipment, plus a large Field Communion Kit which was even larger than my original suitcase. I didn't have a car, public transport would be difficult, and I couldn't scrounge a lift as no one else on the course was posted to Scotland. My problem was solved when one of the medical officers on the course announced that she was selling her ten-year-old Vauxhall Viva. Having been posted to BAOR (British Army of the Rhine) a spanking new tax-free Volvo estate was awaiting her collection. (Volvo estates were very popular among army officers in the 70s and 80s. "What is the difference between a Volvo estate and a hedgehog?" soldiers would jokingly ask. Answer – "Hedgehogs have the pricks on the outside!" – reflecting the love-hate relationship which often existed between the officer corps and the rank and file.)

I used my first military pay cheque to buy my transportation for the 400-mile trek to Redford Barracks in Edinburgh, where Christine and nine-month-old Barbara had already moved into our first army married quarter at 5 Redford Gardens. And so I arrived at my first unit of attachment and at my first church, St Margaret's Garrison Church, ready to serve out my Probationary Period.

We actually only spent 18 months based in Edinburgh, but these months were filled with a surprising array of new experiences and unique opportunities. I led the chaplains onto parade when HRH Princess Margaret presented 1st Battalion Royal Highland Fusiliers (Princess Margaret's Own Glasgow and Ayrshire Regiment) with new colours to mark their tercentenary, I was marooned on a desert island in the Caribbean, I learnt how to "perambulate" with the other officers in front of the whole battalion of men, I appeared briefly on BBC TV Evening News when we were mobilised to put out fires in Glasgow and I hooked for the Royal Highland Fusiliers when we defeated the King's Own Scottish Borderers in the first round of the Army Rugby Cup in the most violent game of rugby of my long rugby-playing career.

I had arrived. I was now Reverend Stephen A Blakey CF. Chaplain to the Forces Class 4 and Padre to 1 RHF. I am still not sure about the accuracy of my father's statement, "They won't take just anybody," but they took me for one! And it took them 40 years to get rid of me!

Chapter 2
The Chaplains' Department

"Zeal in his profession and good sense, gentle manner, a distinctive and impressive manner of reading Divine Service; a firm constitution of body as well as of mind." – The qualifications for a chaplain at the time of the founding of the Army Chaplains' Department by Royal Warrant in 1796.

By the time I joined up as one of the new intake chaplains for 1977, the Chaplains' Department had been in existence for over one hundred and eighty years and during those two centuries had evolved into an effective organisation which provided and supported Christian chaplaincy to the British army in all its different structures: Regular, Territorial and Cadet. The Chaplains' Department, ike every other part of military life, has its rules, protocols and traditions which feel as if they have been there for ever, since Adam was a boy, but which in reality are very much just the latest expression of how things ought to be done. Nothing in the military stays the same for long. The pressure of military requirements, the views of society, the politics of the government and, quite simply, the finances available, mean that change is always a fact of life. What might seem to have 'aye been' is probably just the latest pragmatic expression of how to get the job done.

Even the definition of the job to be done changes with time. Back in my early days as an army chaplain we had RAChD pencils with the strap line 'To make and sustain Christians.' By the end of my 40 years' service very few of my colleagues would have seen that as a primary goal of chaplaincy, and it certainly was not official policy of MOD Chaplains. 'Convergence' and 'all-souls-ministry' were still a long way off.

The idea of a career path never entered my mind in those early days. It would be too strong to say that I had just drifted into this sphere of ministry but certainly fair to highlight my lack of long-term planning. My initial appointment was for three years. I was extremely content with the way things had turned out so far, and I was open to seeing how it might all develop.

Having said that, I was soon drawn into a mentality of wondering where my next posting would take me, and an awareness that the then annual Confidential Reports (now OJAR – Officers' Joint Appraisal Report) shaped every officer's promotions and postings, and before I knew it, I was as interested in the progress of my own military career as all my colleagues were in theirs. In many ways this went against Church of Scotland understanding of ministry. There are no bishops in our church, so in theory all kirk ministers are equal, though as they say, "some are more equal than others". Without a doubt there is a hierarchy within the Kirk, with some ministers' opinions carrying considerably more weight than those of others. I think we Church of Scotland army chaplains did feel a sense of superiority over our Anglican brothers for whom climbing up the greasy pole was, in our opinion, in their DNA.

For me this opinion was reinforced when for a few months I covered a vacant post that had been filled previously by a Church of England colleague. I was intrigued by the contents of his filing cabinet. It would be normal to leave behind sufficient paperwork to ensure that the incoming chaplain can settle-in easily and quickly get a feel for how things function in his new unit. To my total surprise, the files were totally empty with the exception of half a dozen letters from various senior local clergy complimenting the previous chaplain on his sterling contribution to various ecumenical events, and an old photocopy of a page from the Army List with details of the Officers of the Royal Army Chaplains Department with their dates of commission and promotion. The latter was covered with all sorts of scribbling indicating the careful attention-to-detail with which my predecessor had been keeping an eye on everyone else's career prospects. The said chaplain did not manage to climb very much further up the greasy pole despite his diligence.

I soon became aware that there was a number of basic factors that would go a long way towards shaping my career path. I had signed up for a three-year short service commission. During this time, I would serve in two locations, possibly with two different units. This would give both me and the Department the opportunity to see if I was suited to this kind of life and ministry. If that all went well, I would be offered a two-year extension to my short service commission. Towards the end of the fifth year there would be a further discussion about whether or not the army would offer me a regular commission. Having joined up at just over twenty-four years of age, a regular commission would give me a total of twenty-six years as an army chaplain, with the option to leave earlier through PVR (Premature Voluntary Retirement) with a pension after sixteen years onwards. It all looked very attractive.

When the time came for me to have the discussion regarding taking a regular commission, I was serving with 1st Battalion, the King's Own Scottish Borderers (KOSB) in Osnabruck as part of the British Army of the Rhine (BAOR). I was invited to meet with Rev Jim Harkness who at that time was the senior Church of Scotland chaplain based in Germany. By the date of our planned meeting, Jim was in fact lying flat on his back in the British Military Hospital in Rinteln (one of ten previous BMHs) having had some major surgery on his spine. Despite his medical situation, the meeting went ahead as planned.

After some brief opening polite conversation at his bedside, Jim came straight to the point. "Stephen, we would like you to consider accepting a regular commission in the department."

"Well, I am certainly very interested," I replied. "What would happen to me if I did go regular?" I think I knew the answers to all the questions about length of service and pensions and promotions and so on and was much more interested to know about my short-term posting prospects.

"If you decide to stay in, you will be posted to Hong Kong next month."

This was beyond my wildest dreams. My wife, Christine, had heard lots of wonderful stories about Hong Kong through her merchant seaman brother Eric and a couple of previous sailor boyfriends, and we had both just read the book *Chasing the Dragon* by missionary Jackie Pullinger. Hong Kong was in our minds and Christine had been praying for us to be posted there. These prayers were driven by a conviction that God had told her that we would go to Hong Kong. I have sometimes suspected that the possibility of getting to Hong Kong was a major factor in her encouraging me to join the army in the first place.

We had been pretty disappointed a few months back when news filtered through that my colleague John Murdoch had been posted to the Far East on a two-year tour as Padre to 1st Battalion Scots Guards. There only was one posting slot for a junior chaplain in Hong Kong, and John would now fill it for the next two years. It might be many years before another Scottish unit would serve in the Far East. In fact, the next Jock unit to go out was the Black Watch, who covered the handover of the Province to the Chinese in 1997.

No Scottish unit in any given garrison really meant that no Scottish chaplain would be based there. Since the early nineteenth century, the Church of Scotland had actively worked to ensure that the pastoral care of its members serving in the forces of the Crown at home and overseas was catered for. Efforts to ensure that the Church of Scotland chaplains were granted equal status with the clergy of the Church of England came later and over a long period of time.

When I was commissioned the primary focus of the ministry of Church of Scotland chaplains in the army was very much to look after the spiritual needs of Scottish soldiers and their families. I believe at that time there were actually more Scots serving outside Scottish units than within them, but there was no doubt that the Scottish battalions and regiments provided a concentration of Church of Scotland personnel and, therefore, were the most sensible places to locate ministers of the Kirk. There were seven Scottish infantry battalions, two battalions of foot guards, two gunner regiments and a tank regiment. In addition to this we had training depots in Aberdeen and Penicuik and a garrison church in Aldershot. All of these required a fulltime chaplain and on top of this, and on top of all of us, sat the Assistant Chaplain General HQ Scotland (army). These sixteen chaplaincy slots could at that time be filled only by the Church of Scotland (and our sister denominations, principally the Presbyterian Church of

Ireland). This had a major influence on the posting plot and on the shaping of our careers.

The chaplaincy posting plot often seemed to be a bit of a mystery to those of us on the receiving end of the posting orders, but it was claimed that it was really much simpler than any of us could imagine. The Deputy Chaplain General, based at MOD Chaplains (Army) took the lead in overseeing the postings of chaplains. Early each morning the cleaner would throw open the windows of the DCG's office. The incoming breeze would ruffle the metal edged circular cardboard discs which were arranged so carefully on the pinboard opposite the DCG's desk. Some would fall to the floor and, before hoovering the carpet, the cleaner would replace the discs, each bearing the name of a chaplain, back onto the board. If your disk ended up in a different place from which it had fallen, you were about to receive a posting order.

As Church of Scotland chaplains we had the protection of the ACG HQ Scotland who, as the leader of our clan of chaplains, exercised particular control over our postings and, on behalf of the Kirk, had a responsibility to ensure that all the Scottish units and posts were, as far as humanly possible, filled by Presbyterian ministers at all times. The number of chaplains for each denomination was based on a ratio of one chaplain for each 1,100 personnel enlisted belonging to that denomination. The very large number of Scots throughout the army resulted in sufficient chaplains to cover these 16 primary posts.

The Church of Scotland was firmly part of the unified chaplains' Department but did sit slightly to the side, enjoying a unique position within the overall structure and privileges, which admittedly came at a cost; most clearly illustrated by the fact that one of us could never be chaplain general.

The Creedy Report of May 1920, which addressed the future administration of the RAChD in the light of lessons learned from the First World War, agreed that the military administration of the RAChD, for denominations other than Roman Catholic, should be undertaken by the Chaplain General. Prior to 1987 it was always assumed that the Chaplain General would be a Church of England clergyman. In the late nineteenth and early twentieth centuries there had been some discomfort with the idea of Church of Scotland chaplains serving under an Anglican Chaplain General, and at one stage the idea of a Presbyterian Chaplain General had been suggested, but in 1927 the Presbyterian churches agreed that it was sufficient that the Deputy Chaplain General (DCG) would be a Presbyterian very second term. This appointment would alternate with the Methodist and United Board chaplains. The first Deputy Chaplain General to be appointed in 1920, as a result of Creedy, was Church of Scotland minister Rev W Stevenson Affray.

When John Whitton, Peter Howson and I met at Bagshot Park in September 1977, the three newest non-Anglican and non-Roman Catholic chaplains, we discussed which of us might become DCG. All things being equal I could serve for 26 years, John for 24 and Peter for 20. There was a fair chance that one of us would achieve this senior position. It was actually John Whitton who made it to the top. John, who in that same conversation, declared his disbelief in the process of 'bulling brogues'. Most of those who served with John over his long career would confirm that he never did get into the 'spit and polish' side of military life. In the same conversation our Methodist colleague Peter Howson expressed high hopes of not only becoming DCG, but possibly also the first Methodist Chaplain General. He made neither post but does continue to play a significant role as an expert in military history. As for me? Well, read on.

In the meantime, my hopes of getting to Hong Kong, which had been badly damaged when John Murdoch received his posting order to go there during his initial short-term commission, were suddenly greatly enhanced when John made the decision to leave the army at the end of his first three years. The fact that the powers-to-be were pretty annoyed with John waiting to the last minute to resign and so ensuring himself six months in the Far East didn't really concern me. Some say that he waited until he was boarding the British Caledonian flight bound for Hong Kong before showing his hand. I confess that I really didn't care. I was thrilled, and when Jim Harkness indicated that in the event of my accepting a regular commission, I would replace John, I accepted immediately.

It was in Hong Kong that I received promotion to CF3 (Chaplain to the Forces Class 3) and changed my Captain's three pips for a Major's crown. Chaplains are non-combatants and purposely do not hold rank in the same way as other members of the army. Newly commissioned chaplains hold the rank of chaplain to the Forces, Class 4 and wear the rank slides of a Captain. This works pretty well. Newly commissioned doctors, vets and lawyers are also all given the rank of Captain.

At tri-service chaplaincy meetings our Royal Navy colleagues will always bring up the fact that while army and RAF chaplains wear rank, RN chaplains do not. They have a habit of informing anyone who will listen to them that this avoids rank being a barrier between a chaplain and the personnel and dependant they are serving, allowing the chaplain to take the same rank as the person the are talking to. I guess our response would be that I have never heard a Nav chaplain call a rating 'Sir' though I am sure that is how he addressed the Rea Admiral. RN chaplains wear officers' uniforms, eat in the wardroom, live i officers' married quarters and send their children to private boarding schools lik all the other officers. Rank only becomes a problem for an army chaplain whe one misuses or abuses his status. Everyone knows we are officers, and havin rank makes it much easier to fit in to the hierarchy which is an inherent part c military life.

Promotion for army chaplains takes them from CF4 which equates t Captain, to CF3 which equates to Major, to CF2 which is Lieutenant Colonel an to CF1 which equates to Colonel. At the top of the tree, we have the Chaplai General (Major General) and Deputy Chaplain General (Brigadier).

Despite my forty years' service I never made it above CF3. I was too youn as a regular, and too old as a reservist. Promotion to CF3 was pretty automatic a the six-year point for regular chaplains, but thereafter promotion was on meri and to some extent 'dead men's shoes'. Back in the 70s and 80s promotion fron CF3 to CF2 could only be achieved after a minimum of twelve years' servic and at the of age forty-two or above. I left the regular army after sixteen years aged 40, and so was too young to be promoted, and the opportunity for reserv chaplains to gain promotion above CF3 only came into existence after I turne 60 and so I was too old to be considered. I now have no rank at all but have th lovely title of Staff Chaplain Scotland as an Officiating Chaplain to the Militar (OCM), which is a civilian position.

When the first of our intake group was informed of his promotion to CF2 h was very excited. Peter Howson, who very seldom phoned any of us, called Johr Whitton and in a somewhat wandering conversation, in which he attempted t disguise his purpose, he discovered that John had not yet been promoted and tha in fact was still too young, and that I was even younger. Peter's thunder was t some extent stolen.

Army chaplaincy has a long history and, like much else in military life i constantly evolving and reinventing itself in order to be more effective anc relevant. It has been a long journey and it seems that most major pragmatic changes were introduced post-campaign as a result of reviewing what had, anc had not, worked in the heat of conflict.

Armies have, of course, had their holy men and priests since the beginning of warfare itself, and Anglican chaplains had been awarded commissions since the Restoration, from 1662 onwards. These clergy, who were appointed by a particular Regiment, were usually attached to the staffs of the Commanders in Chief which meant that they were pretty well removed from the rank and file, but they were at least witnesses to many of the campaigns and, because they were well educated men with good literary skills, they were often the ones who wrote the vivid and well-detailed accounts of the conflicts.

In 1796 these posts of Regimental chaplain, with chaplains appointed by the individual regiments, were abolished in favour of a regular Corps of chaplains which was established by Royal Warrant. The aim of the Royal Warrant was to provide the army with a number of clerics who were sufficiently well paid to enable them to minister to the forces overseas on foreign service. The King hoped that 'more effectual provision may be made for the regular performance of religious duties throughout the army, without bringing any additional charge upon the public'.

The qualifications laid down in 1796 were: *'Zeal in his profession and good sense, gentle manner, a distinctive and impressive manner of reading Divine Service; a firm constitution of body as well of mind.'*

Although the Royal Warrant was granted in 1796 and was designed to apply to the whole army it was some time before churches other than the Church of England were fully recognised, and it took a good number of years for the Army Chaplains' Department to become what we would now deem as 'fit for purpose'. The Duke of Wellington, for example, complained of the shortage of chaplains to tend to the spiritual needs of his army. He blamed poor pay and conditions, and so he improved these and thereby oversaw a consequential rise in the number of young ministers joining his forces in the Peninsular War (1808–1814).

Further progress was made in 1844 when Rev Dr George Robert Gleig was appointed Principal Chaplain to the Forces. He went on to lay the foundations for a modern Chaplains' Department within the British army, but the development was slow and during the Crimean War (1853–1856) there was still a great shortage of chaplains. The conditions in the Crimea were dreadful and the chaplaincy cover was totally inadequate. A public outcry resulted in a national newspaper appeal for more clergymen, who would serve as assistant chaplains for the hospitals in Scutari and the camps in the Crimea. This resulted in a total of sixty chaplains going to the Crimea – twelve of whom died. These were largely supported financially by the Society for the Propagation of th Gospel.

One of those who responded to this call for additional chaplains was predecessor in my present parish. In 1855 the Rev Francis Nicoll Cannan, th then minister of Lintrathen in Angus, volunteered to assist with chaplaincy to th troops. Mr Cannan was one of nine Presbyterian ministers sent out to Crimea He served with the 72nd Highlanders with responsibility for the hospitals a Balaklava. It appears that army chaplaincy appealed to him for, on his return, h accepted one of the new commissions into the Army Chaplains' Department o 1 July 1858, but with his commission antedated to April 1855 in recognition o his services in the Crimea.

He served in the army for 20 years, ending up as a chaplain to the Force Class 1 (full Colonel) and retiring on half pay in 1875. Rev Cannan is mentione in the history of the St Andrews Garrison Church, Aldershot, where he is name as the first Presbyterian minister of The Iron Church (known by the soldiers a the 'Tin Tabernacle').

After the Crimean War, the Chaplain General of the period, Dr G R Gleig attempted to organise the Department on more efficient lines. The Army List o October 1856 shows the chaplain general, twenty chaplains and thirty-five assistant chaplains.

Rev H P Wright, who had served as the senior army chaplain in the Crimea suggested in his very full letter to the Secretary of State for War in 1858 that every unit should have its own chaplain, and also that provision should be made for Presbyterians and Roman Catholics. "Give to every Highland Regiment its Presbyterian chaplain; and to the Roman Catholics a body of priests in proportion to the number of Roman Catholics in our army."

In his reckoning the establishment of the Army Chaplains' Department to look after an army of 145,000 souls should be 92 Church of England, 25 Roman Catholics and 8 Presbyterians.

The Department was originally made up entirely of the Established Church clergy from the Church of England, but this clearly did not represent the ecclesiastical mix of the army's personnel. Members of other churches put pressure on the Department and slowly, over some years, chaplains from other denominations were authorised. The first group to succeed was the Roman Catholics in 1836. They were followed by the Presbyterians in 1858, Wesleyans in 1881 and Jews in 1892.

The above reference to the Established Church is a reminder, of course, that the Church of Scotland is the equivalent to an Established Church north of the border, and as such was bound to have an opinion on all sorts of matters relating to its own clergy and the spiritual welfare of Scots serving in the British army.

To ensure all of this was done correctly a Committee on Chaplains to HM Forces was established in 1860. It would not only look after the interest of the Presbyterian chaplains and their Churches' members serving in the armed forces but also defend the position of the national Church within the military in Scotland and abroad. Its remit was to attend to the spiritual wants of soldiers and sailors, and to correspond with army chaplains. Dr John Cook of St Andrews was its first Convenor. It is said that one of his first tasks was to shorten the name to The Committee for Army and Navy Chaplains, but I can assure you that when I joined in 1977 it was still known by its full name, The Church of Scotland Committee on Chaplains to HM Forces, though it does seem now to have been shortened to Forces Chaplains' Committee in the present Church of Scotland Yearbook.

From the early days the defence of the status of the Kirk and its ministers and their people was regarded as important and The Committee found itself being forced to take a strong role in defending the rights of its chaplains. One such issue was the idea that Presbyterian ministers would come under the authority of an Anglican chaplain general. In 1864 a letter was received from Earl de Grey, then Secretary of State for War, stating that "the chaplain general (who was, of course, Church of England) will cease for the future to exercise any supervision over the Presbyterian chaplains of the army". The argument rumbled on for decades until the agreed rotation of the DCG appointment mentioned above was confirmed in the late 1920s.

The introduction of substantial changes to the structure of chaplaincy after Crimea set a pattern of review and reform after other major conflicts, and the First World War was no exception to this. The First World War offered a huge challenge to the Department. In August 1914 the army chaplains Department had 117 chaplains (89 Church of England, 11 Presbyterian and 17 Roman Catholic). These numbers expanded rapidly in keeping with the size and demands of the military operation and by August 1918 the number had risen to 3,474.

Church of England 1985
Roman Catholic 649
Presbyterian 302

Wesleyan 256

United Board 251

Jewish 16

Welsh Calvinist 10

Salvation army 5

(United Board chaplains came from the Baptist, Congregationalist, Primitive Methodist and United Methodist churches)

The war challenged previously held ideas about how military chaplains spent their time. When based at home in the UK it was easy to maintain a set routine of church parades and services, visits to the sick in hospital, and so on. Once on the move, or at the front line, it was a completely different situation and environment. Many chaplains found themselves helping out in ways they had not expected, especially when it came to supporting the work of those clearing casualties and caring for the wounded. These men of God who found themselves in the midst of the horrors of war were faced with a whole range of new challenges.

Being non-combatants did not mean that they escaped the reality of the battlefield. They were often exposed to exactly the same conditions and dangers that faced the armed soldiers – possibly greater, considering that they were unarmed and were expected to provide an example for the men to follow. Their duties often went well beyond their spiritual brief, and they would frequently find themselves acting as advocates for improvements in the general welfare of all the troops, and doing their bit to raise the morale of the men in extremely difficult and hazardous conditions.

Reports of chaplaincy on the Western Front varied greatly, but the overall feeling was that the chaplains had risen to the challenge. This was recognised after the end of the war when an Army Order (No. 92) published on 22 February 1919 read as follows:

His Majesty the King, in view of the splendid work which has been performed by the Army Chaplains' Department during the present War, has been graciously pleased to approve of the Department being in future designated The Royal Army Chaplains' Department.

In February 2019 The Royal Army Chaplains' Department celebrated, in the presence of Her Majesty the Queen, the centenary of the granting of the Royal prefix to the Army Chaplains' Department by her Queen's grandfather King George. The centenary service was held in The Guards Chapel on Birdcage Walk in London.

Reading the accounts of those who have served over the centuries, it is clear that while much has changed, and continues to change in the fluidity of modern life, the challenge of chaplaincy remains much the same, finding a place and role, being available for spiritual duties and ministry opportunities, while being a useful contributor to unit life results in all sorts of tasks and functions coming the chaplain's way. And for me much of those were shaped like a rugby ball.

Chapter 3
Rugby

"Rugby is the closest you'll get to going to war. You are playing a very physica game and you look after each other." – Will Carling, ex Royal Regiment c Wales, former Captain of England Rugby.

As we hunkered down for the first set scrum of the afternoon, the tight head prop turned his head towards me and quietly said in my ear, "Thank the Lord we are on the same side this time Padre!" This was a huge compliment. Cpl Lundy KOSB was probably still bearing the scars – physical and emotional – from the game a few weeks earlier on the rugby park outside Fort George, Inverness when the 1st Bn Royal Highland Fusiliers knocked 1st Bn Kings Own Scottish Borderers out of the first round of the Army Rugby Cup. This was very much a case of a mainly football-playing battalion beating a strongly rugby-playing battalion at their own game in front of their own support.

It was a bruising affair, probably the most violent game of rugby I have ever played in and the resulting victory by 1RHF (who that year were the Army Football Cup champions) has gone down in history. Every now and then members of the RHF team bump into each other, and the story is retold. Most recently, in the spring of 2019, while conducting the funeral of a Territorial Army veteran, I was approached by a soldier who had played with me in the RHF in the match and who wanted to reminisce. The memories live on.

My first experience of the game of rugby was at Station Park, St Andrews in late August 1964. My parents had just bought a new house and we were in the process of moving from Glasgow to Fife. I was the only new boy in the Primary 7 class of Madras College. It was in the days when most of the posher schools in Scotland seemed to play rugby. Something to do with the saying that 'rugby is the ruffians' game played by gentlemen, while football is the gentleman's game played by ruffians.' At that stage of my academic life in St Andrews we had no choice. We all played rugby.

So, there I was kitted out in my spanking new rugby kit, old style navy Scotland top with white collar, white shorts, navy blue socks and a pair of slightly dodgy second-hand boots. I don't know who the boots had been handed down from, but they gave me my first experience of cobbling. They were leather soled with studs hammered into the thick soles. I spent many an evening with a hammer and a metal last making sure that I had sufficient studs in place while trying to avoid the nails sticking right through and puncturing my feet. It was a great joy when I was bought my first pair of modern boots with the studs already moulded into the sole. The alternative of course was screw-in studs, which allowed you the option varying the length of your studs depending on the weather. Long thin studs would give better grip on a muddy surface while short fat ones would be more comfortable on a rock-hard pitch.

On my first games afternoon at Madras College I gathered with the rest of the class waiting for the arrival of C.C. MacLeod, the PE teacher and rugby coach. Looking down at the group of scrawny eleven-year-olds he asked, "What sort of game is rugby?" Keen to get some attention I shot my hand up. "Well, Blakey?" he asked.

"It's a rough game, sir!" I replied enthusiastically, only to be outdone by John Darroch, the same John Darroch who a decade later would point me towards military chaplaincy, who declared with a victorious smirk on his face:

"No, it is a handling game, Mr MacLeod!"

I guess I should have known better than to speak out. Everyone else had been playing rugby for a year by this time and would have learnt all the correct answers to Mr MacLeod's questions. I had a lot to learn in all sorts of ways, but a year later when we started proper competitive games against other schools, I was appointed Captain of 1st Year Rugby, so I must have picked up something. That first year of games was pretty successful on the whole. We lost only two games, the first and last games of the season which were both against Waid Academy from Anstruther. We did get our revenge however when we played a fifteen minutes each-way match against the Waid to provide some entertainment between the semi-finals and the final of the Midland Schools Rugby Sevens tournament. We beat them that day, and on every other day we were drawn against them for the rest of my time as a pupil at Madras. We did like thrashing the Waid!

I played rugby throughout my school days, during my university education at St Andrews (where I captained the Bejants XV – 1971-72) and Edinburgh (where I played with Edinburgh Wanderers), and then played or coached throughout most of my regular army career. Sport plays an important part in military life and rugby provided an opportunity for me to be actively involved in a useful way with the troops.

The importance of being out there and participating on sports afternoon was highlighted for me well before I actually joined up, during my interview with the Church of Scotland Committee on Chaplains to HM Forces. This committee of the Kirk plays an important part in the selection and oversight of ministers of the Church of Scotland who become army chaplains. Their recommendation to the chaplain general, as representative of the 'sending church' or 'authorising authority' in my day pretty much made up the CG's mind about who should or should not be allowed into the Department. Much has changed since the 1970s and potential chaplains are now required to pass officer selection like everyone else. Those of us who came into the department prior to the rigour of today do sometimes wonder if we would have been accepted now using the updated process.

I had arrived a little late for the interview with the Chaplains' Committee and so was somewhat on edge. The interview was held in an austere lawyer's office in Charlotte Square, Edinburgh. Very Edinburgh, very grand, and very daunting for a 23-year-old theology student. In due course I was ushered in to the gathering of senior gentlemen in serious looking dark suits and old school ties. The interview was more of a conversation than a traditional interview, and I felt that I sailed through a whole range of fairly relevant topics until we got to discuss how I might imagine myself spending Wednesday afternoons. It is hard to believe that how I expressed my intentions for Wednesday afternoon activities probably influenced whether or not I became an army chaplain.

For those who are a bit mystified by the importance of Wednesdays between the hours of 13:00 and 17:00 let me explain with the two simple words *Sports Afternoon*. Since the beginning of time it has been a tradition in the British army to play sports on a Wednesday afternoon. All sorts of sports at all sorts of levels, and all part of getting and staying fit, building team spirit, and displaying your own unit's prowess over as many other military units as possible. All of this reflecting the public-school ethos brought into the army by the officer class.

And so, the question, which the committee were building up to, was what would I as Padre be doing on a Wednesday afternoon. "How are you as a football referee?" one of them asked. Well, I had never refereed a game of football, and really hadn't played much football at all except the occasional kick-about with my brothers in the back garden. We had a sort of family tradition that after our evening meal at home I would take on the three young ones for a game on the back lawn. For me the advantage was that I avoided washing or drying the dishes, and for everyone else it tired the youngsters out prior to bedtime.

I think the only competitive game I ever played in, well apart from a few years in primary school as a cub scout, was one Sunday afternoon in St Andrews. I was lounging around St Regulus Hall common room after Sunday lunch and was far too relaxed to manage to say 'no!' when a few members of the hall football team came looking for someone to make up their eleven for a match against St Salvator's Hall in the intra-mural football league. I was dragged off to the sports fields and told that my task was to shadow Marshall someone-or-other in the opposing team. He was by far their star player, and if we could starve him of possession, we would probably win the game.

As a rugby forward, I was pretty used to just following the ball, so I set my sights on this guy and annoyed the hell out of him for the next hour and a half.

37

Everywhere he went I was there pestering and tackling. We won, and I was a bit of a hero, though perhaps not to this guy who I later discovered was a member of the University 1st XI football team.

"How are you as a football referee?"

"Well, I play rugby, and I would hope to continue doing so in the army, so guess that is what I would see myself doing most Wednesdays."

I could tell straight away that this wasn't the response that was being looked for. "But you could referee a football match?"

It took me a couple of more exchanges before waking up to the fact that the correct answer was "Yes, of course I could do so."

We had almost lost sight of the real question, which was about getting involved with the men, and the opportunity that sport provided for this. There is much in a soldier's normal daily activity in which the chaplain cannot take part and some of it to be purposefully avoided.

When I arrived in Redford Barracks in the late Autumn of 1977 Padre John Stewart, who had been appointed as my 'bishop' during my first year by way of making up for my lack of Probationary Period, took me into the barracks to introduce me to various members of the battalion. He asked the Company Commander of Headquarters Company, Major Andy Stewart, if he could give me some advice about a daily routine.

"What time would you expect Stephen to come into barracks in the morning, for example?"

Andy's advice was suitably vague but laced with some wisdom. "Well, best not to come in too early when all the shouting is going on. Wait until Orders are over. Come in about 08:30 hours and spend an hour walking round all the companies and departments so that folk see you and know that you are at work and available if they need you. Go to the officers' mess for coffee at 10:00 hours and then really for the rest of the day it's up to you what you get up to."

The most important element of wisdom in all of this was, "Wait until Orders are over." Orders are when soldiers who have misbehaved are dealt with. The individuals are marched in front of whichever officer is dealing with their misdemeanour, there is a lot of shouting of commands and stamping of feet, punishments are dispensed, and the miscreants are marched off to get on with the day's tasks or to be incarcerated in the Guard Room. Not the place for a peace-loving man of God to be found.

Throughout forty years of military service I managed pretty well to avoid getting caught up in the fury of daily Orders, and the one time I did forget served to refresh my memory for years to come. I needed to see the Chief Clerk about having an order of service printed for a special church service and wandered into Battalion Headquarters in the middle of Commanding Officer's Orders. The sight of eight soldiers dressed in service dress, bare headed, standing at attention and looking scared outside the CO's office should have been enough to warn me off, but I continued down the corridor. As I passed the office, the door flew open, the air was filled with "Right, left, right, left!" and a wee soldier with the Regimental Sergeant Major on his heels marched at an incredibly quick pace out of the office, across the corridor and straight into the broom cupboard opposite. The broom cupboard door slammed shut, the RSM barked loudly for about ten seconds, the door flew open and the two occupants returned to the office, where the soldier accepted the commanding officer's punishment.

I should point out that this was in 1981, and the exercise of military discipline has changed considerably in the intervening decades. When that particular officer took over command of his battalion, he locked up two soldiers at his first commanding officer's orders: one got two days in the guard room on bread and water, and the other five days on bread, water and soup. I think if a commanding officer did that today, he too would find himself locked up.

The 'conversation' in the broom cupboard had been focussed on whether or not the soldier would accept the commanding officer's sentence. There was always the option of requesting to be tried by a higher authority, which in this case would have been the brigade commander but could go all the way up to a court martial. Battalions much preferred to deal with their own soldiers and I suppose to avoid the bad publicity of their dirty washing being aired in public.

Apart from daily orders, there were really only a few other parts of unit life which should ideally be avoided by the padre. The challenge was not so much about what to avoid as to how to become usefully involved. It would be rare for my week to be filled with spiritual or welfare ministry activity, though this did sometime happen. During the quieter times of life, sport provided a wonderful way to be involved on an equal basis with the men and I found rugby especially useful.

My first experience of army rugby was with 1 RHF. As a theology student at New College, Edinburgh, I had joined Edinburgh Wanderers Rugby Club. This was in the days before FP (Former Pupil) Rugby Clubs in Scotland opened up to

allow non-former pupils to play for them. This meant that if you moved t
Edinburgh to study or to work but hadn't gone to school in Edinburgh, the onl
top-level rugby club in the city that you could play for was Edinburg
Wanderers, who were based at Greenside Lodge and played at Murrayfield.
joined them when I was a theology student and was able to continue there durin
my first army posting to 1 RHF in Redford Barracks. There were a few other
from the officers' mess including the CO Lt Col John Drummond, Alan Roberts
Rab Dallas and John Kelly, who also played for Wanderers. So we playe
civilian rugby on Saturday afternoons and military rugby on Wednesda
afternoons.

In 1977, 1 RHF were drawn against 1 KOSB in the first round of the Arm
Rugby Cup and, as I said, people still talk about it. I met John Kelly at an Orde
of St John Festival in 2017, and one of the first topics of conversation was u
beating the Borderers forty years previously.

The match was to be played at Fort George, outside Inverness, and on th
appointed day we set out for the trip north. I had only been with the battalion fo
a few weeks and didn't really know my fellow officers very well, and when the
all arranged for the junior ranks to travel by train while they shared cars, I opte
(or more likely was volunteered!) to accompany the Jocks. You would think tha
travelling with half a dozen or so soldiers by train from Edinburgh to Invernes
would be a safe and trouble-free outing... and I was naïve enough back then t
think so. We boarded the train and settled down in the buffet car. "It was thei
idea, m'lud!"

The buffet didn't open, and when the ticket collector came round after w
had passed through Perth, he explained that there was a bus strike in Glasgow
and the buffet attendant had missed the train. "Nae problem, sir, we could rur
the buffet for you," joked one of the lads. The guard laughed as he left th
carriage, the train turned a curve in the track, and the buffet shutter fell oper
revealing a fully stocked shop... drink and all.

"Rats," I thought, "this cannot be good." There was a buzz of excitement as
my fellow travellers eyed the shelves stacked full of cans of beer, sweets and
crisps... "We're on a winner here!"... "Bevvy time, boys!"... and I prayed tha
the guard would get back here very quickly while trying to suggest to the lads
that it might be just a wee bit too obvious if we arrived drunk at Inverness and
with an empty buffet.

The Police boarded the train at Pitlochry and between there and Aviemore statements were taken, the stock was checked, and our bags were searched. Despite some of the lads having a couple of their own cans of beer secreted away alongside their boots and strips for an after-match refreshment, we left the train in Inverness as free men, and I as a wiser Padre, never to be caught again volunteering to chaperone a group of Scottish soldiers. Well, that was my intention.

The Kings Own Scottish Borderers had a great rugby tradition. They had won the Army Rugby Cup in the early 1960s with Scottish International Brian Shillinglaw and others. The tradition and belief lived on. In the battalion mentality, the prospect of giving 15 members of the Royal Highland Fusiliers a right good seeing to whetted their appetite. Battalion life stopped for the afternoon, and everyone and their dog was ordered out to the sports field to watch the massacre. But the massacre went the wrong way.

Fort George, twelve miles outside Inverness, was built after the 1745–46 Jacobite rebellion to keep the unruly Highlanders at bay. It had never been attacked or seen military action, but that day in 1977 it saw conflict for the first time in two hundred and thirty-two years when a new padre arrived as hooker of 1RHF. It was a no holds barred affair and two Borderers ended up hospital to have broken bones attended to.

Matthew Robertson was the Padre of the KOSB at the time, and he gave me enormous abuse from the touchline. As hooker I was throwing the ball in for the lineouts and so I was the player nearest to the crowd, which of course was made up entirely of Borderers. Matthew took every opportunity to remind them that I was the RHF Padre and all sorts of interesting insults were thrown at me. The abuse was to no avail, and we won the game and the war.

A year later I replaced Matthew in Fort George and soon took over as rugby officer of 1 KOSB. It was an interesting position to be in. The foe had become a friend, though when I took my first training session with the rugby squad on a Friday morning a few weeks later, some of the less fit members were less than friendly in their comments. In my defence, eating a cooked breakfast even an hour before rugby training was pretty likely to end badly. Revisiting your breakfast is never a pleasant experience.

In the interim I had met up with a fair number of the Borderers at Craigiehall, Headquarters of the army in Scotland, where we were training with the army in Scotland Rugby for a forthcoming match against the Royal Navy in Scotland.

They thrashed us but that was possibly due to the fact that many of their team were submariners who had just arrived home from a long trip and had far too much energy and aggression to use up. We were unfortunate to be caught in their path.

Over the coming decade I served as rugby officer for a number of the units served with and hooked for all five of my regular battalions. Rugby provided a wonderful means of mixing with the men, and even although the main contact was with the squad itself the enhanced profile of the Padre helped in my ministry with the hundreds who did not play. Soldiers quite like their chaplain to be something more than just the 'God botherer'. Seeing you doing your stuff on the rugby park made you more human in their eyes.

As rugby officer it wasn't always easy to get the players turned out for a battalion rugby match. Although a major unit was over 600 strong, the actual pool of quality rugby players was often quite small, and the really good players were usually skilled at a wide range of other sports and so were in demand by the other battalion teams. Once leave dates and regimental duties were factored in, the rugby officer often found himself really struggling to turn out a decent team. Having the senior battalion personnel in general, and the commanding officer in particular, on-side was always helpful in ensuring the first choice fifteen players would be released from other calls on their time.

My requests for support from the commanding officer didn't always go smoothly. I was serving with 1st Battalion Scots Guards in Elizabeth Barracks in the autumn of 1984. The commanding officer was Lt Col Kim Ross, one of the nicest men in the British army. Battalion life was often pretty quiet on a Friday afternoon with all the single men and officers who were not on duty at the weekend heading off at lunch time to London or elsewhere, so Friday lunchtimes in the mess had a tendency to drift into 'port afternoons'. After a pleasant lunch in the company of fellow officers and guests, and with no need to rush back to the office, or home to the family, the port decanter would circle more than once or twice, the banter would flow, and we would all enjoy the ambience and the humour.

These lunches did tend to drift towards afternoon teatime, but no one was really paying much attention. Occasionally a member of the Mess staff would approach one of the officers. "Sir, your wife is on the phone and wondering if you are in the mess." She had probably already tried the office phone number with no success, and of course there were no mobile phones in those days. The roblem was that if you owned up to being in the mess then you might be summoned home and that would be the end of the party for you. Mess waiters were known to sometimes return to the telephone to inform the wife concerned that her husband was 'nowhere to be seen'.

It was after one of these lunches, when the CO had gone back to his office to finish off some important business before the weekend, that I decided that I really did need to have a quick chat with him about the struggle I was having to get a good rugby team turned out for the match the following Wednesday.

I headed off to his office with my young cocker spaniel in tow. Having gained entry to that rather unique foot guards' orderly room, which is shared by the commanding officer, second in command, adjutant and assistant adjutant, I saluted smartly and then with the occasional slurred word eloquently poured out my woes, and explained how very important it was for the honour of his battalion that the CO backed me and commanded the company commanders to release the players. It went really well, and Colonel Kim said that he would do as asked. I was really chuffed that I had successfully presented my case and achieved the result I was looking for. I pulled myself up to attention, threw up a smart salute, turned to the right and fell over my dog. The CO smiled quietly at his Padre lying flat on his face, me wondering if perhaps my presentation had suddenly lost its effect.

Being rugby officer opened all sorts of doors. I nominated myself to attend the official army rugby coaching course at Sennelager in Germany. It was a week away from the Battalion, with busy days and relaxing evenings. I was really pleased when I was summoned by our Second in Command, Major Ian Lowis, some weeks later to be informed that I had passed the course, and was in fact top student.

Ian was a key individual when it came to developing the KOSB battalion rugby club in Germany. He held the purse strings, and we had all sorts of plans, most of which required funding. The quartermaster had given us a building to convert into a club house, and that required lots of furniture and decoration. Well, mainly a bar and beer pumps. It ended up being an ideal venue for post-match refreshments. We also managed to persuade the second in command to fund a rugby tour back to Scotland under the partial guise of a KAPE (Keeping the Army in the Public Eye) tour.

Twenty of us headed back to the Scottish borders to play five matches from Berwick-on-Tweed across to Dumfries over a twelve-day period. It was great fun and a great success. We only managed to win one match out of the five which perchance was the one I played in, but we did a great job in maintaining the good reputation of KOSB across our regimental recruiting area.

We even went to church on both Sundays. Attending Duns Parish Church where I would later become parish minister, and then also visiting Coldstream Parish Church where we collected a Baptismal Font which had been gifted to the KOSB Regimental Kirk and needed transported over to Osnabruck.

Having set up the tour I almost didn't manage to go on it. Our family had continued to grow, with Malcolm being born during my time at Redford Barracks, Edinburgh, and Caroline born during my time at Fort George Inverness.

Christine was now due to give birth to our fourth child in about six weeks time, and we had sort of assumed that her mother would fly out to Germany to look after Christine and the other three children while I was gone. I tried very hard to explain to my mother-in-law that leading the battalion rugby tour to Scotland for two weeks was a vital military duty and not just some 'jolly' with my rugby mates. She dug her heels in and refused to fly over, but the day was saved by Sister Barbara Harrop of the Church Army who moved in with Christine for the two weeks.

On my return I was told that Barbara's cooking was not the best in the world, and that the sales of Captain Birdseye's Fish Fingers in the Osnabruck NAAFI had gone through the roof. Christine survived it all and Graham was born a few weeks later.

Ian Lowis' final contribution to the success of the tour was when he authorised the design and purchase of the official tour tie. It was an attractive blue with gold rugby ball motif under which the figures XXV were embroidered. The XXV is for 25, the KOSB being the 25th Regiment of Foot. We wore the tie with pride and used it as a gift to present to the various club officials we met on tour.

That tour tie appeared at Bonkyl Kirk one Sunday in 2015. I had been conducting the baptism of a local farmer's grandchild during the morning service. There were lots of guests, both family and friends, including a fair number of Border farmers, many of whom had played rugby in the days when the mention of names like Hawick, Gala and Kelso, would have struck fear into many rugby players from further north. I certainly recall Saturday visits to the Borders. We would travel south from Edinburgh thinking that perhaps this time result would be different, only to reflect on the way home that, once the naesthetic power of the beer had worn off, the disappointment of losing would e multiplied by the aches and pains of a bruising encounter on the rugby park.

I was shaking hands with the departing congregation as they left the church fter the baptism when I noticed one guy wearing our 1982 rugby tour tie. That's an interesting tie!"

"Aye, I got it playing for Kelso against the KOSBs when they came on a rugby tour ages ago. I think their minister was in charge of it all." I was able to tell him that it was in 1982 and that I was the minister in charge, and he was able to remind me that we had arrived with a number of substitute players changed and ready to be used, only to be informed that Scottish Rugby had not yet changed the laws to allow substitutes and that they might as well get changed back into civvies. Our fifteen men put up a good fight but were well beaten by the fifteen men of Kelso, though we did match up to them pretty well in the clubhouse afterwards.

Overseas most of our rugby was played against other military teams, so it was great to have the opportunity to travel back home to find some civilian competition. Rugby is played in Germany, and the national team was formed in

1927, but I don't recall us ever playing any local teams during my three posting there.

Chapter 4
The German Experience

"When you move from one country to another you have to accept that there are some things that are better and some things that are worse, and there is nothing you can do about it." – Bill Bryson

My experience of visiting other countries was remarkably limited. I attended boarding school in Atlanta, Georgia, USA for two terms during my final year of secondary school and had a marvellous time while escaping the demands of sixth year exams. It was not quite a gap-year, but near enough. I then fell in love with and married a Norwegian, well half-Norwegian, girl whose parents owned a summer hytte just outside Kristiansand on the southern tip of Norway, which meant that I got to spend a few weeks each year in the idyllic beauty of Scandinavia. When my posting to Germany as part of the British Army of the

Rhine was confirmed I really was very excited by the opportunity to explor
another country.

The British Army of the Rhine (BAOR) was home from home for thousand
of British soldiers and their families throughout most of the twentieth century
There have in fact been two formations named British Army of the Rhine, both
were originally occupation forces in Germany, one after the First World War
and the other after the Second World War. When the original BAOR wa
disbanded in 1929 no one could have imagined that it would be firmly back in
position sixteen years later.

The second British Army of the Rhine, the one to which I was posted in 1980
was formed on 25 August 1945 from the British Liberation Army. After the end
of the Second World War it was agreed that Germany should be divided into four
zones of occupation – British, American, French and Russian. Similar
arrangements were agreed for Austria and for the City of Berlin, which wa
otherwise deep in East Germany (The Russian Zone of Occupation). This BAOR
occupational force consisted of 80,000 personnel. Its original function was to
support the military government which would administer the British zone of
occupied Germany. In due course when the German people themselves took over
the government of their own nation its role reduced to being the command
formation for the British troops based in Germany.

During the Cold War the potential threat of Soviet invasion across the North
German Plain into West Germany increased, and BAOR became more
responsible for the defence of West Germany than for its occupation.

I spent six of my sixteen years' regular service in Germany. This would have
been a fairly normal ratio for infantry soldiers, and I was with infantry for my
whole time, but soldiers serving with armoured and artillery units often spent
almost their whole careers based there. My three tours in Germany were with
Kings Own Scottish Borderers in Osnabruck and the with Royal Scots in Werl,
both as part of BAOR, and with the Black Watch in West Berlin prior to the Wall
coming down.

In the summer of 1964, I had sat with my father in the assembly hall of
Madras College, St Andrews. I was about to start secondary school and there
were some major decisions to be made regarding the subjects I would study.
Well, I say decisions because I assume that there was more than one, though the
only one I can actually remember was whether to choose German or Russian as
my modern language. I was in the two-language stream and as I remember it,

part from this, everyone pretty much took the same subjects with little choice
in year one and year two. We all had to study Latin but we could choose to learn
German, which unusually was the main foreign language taught at Madras at that
time, or opt for Russian. French was studied by the one-language stream, and
Spanish was offered as an option in later years. From a two-language class of
fifty pupils, only four of us chose Russian.

With the benefit of hindsight, I should really have chosen German. Some
understanding of German would have been really useful when reading Old
Testament at New College. Terms like 'Heilsgeschichte' were common in our
textbooks. My theology studies would also have benefitted greatly if I had kept
Latin going for more than two years, instead of taking the easy option of applied
mechanics (which I could probably have passed at the end of one year of the two-
year course.) Years later, as I struggled to learn some basic German so that I
could pass the Army Colloquial German Speaker Course, I wondered if my
father had got it wrong.

Not that my Russian was completely wasted. I did achieve an O Level pass
and from time to time have managed to use the odd phrase. Conversing with the
Russians on the British Military Train from West Berlin to West Germany, for
example, and also when studying Serbian in Sarajevo many years later. One of
the results of the inter-ethnic breakdown in Bosnia-Herzegovina in the 1990s
was that the blended language of Serbo-Croat had become once again two
separate languages of Serbian and Croatian. At one time all the children in
Sarajevo would have gone to school together but since then they had their own
single ethnic school classes and their own textbooks. My friend Bill Common
and I took night classes in Serbian (or was it Croatian?) during our months
together in Camp Butmir, Sarajevo.

Bill and I had originally served together in Redford Barracks in 1977. He
carried the Queen's Colour on the Royal Highland Fusiliers Tercentenary
Parade. We met up again in Butmir Camp in Sarajevo when he was on the staff
of HQ EUFOR and was my Kirk Elder for Church of Scotland services on the
camp.

Perhaps the main benefit of my Russian school classes was the ability to read
the Cyrillic alphabet which was used on the road signs in Republika Srpska, the
Serbian region of Bosnia Herzegovina. Our British drivers frequently got totally
lost because they had no idea what the road signs said, couldn't read the names

of the towns and villages, and so struggled to follow the directions. It was one of the few times that they found it very helpful to have the padre around.

My lack of German language skills was seldom a problem, however, during the three postings in Germany. The British military had its own barracks, its own housing areas, its own schools, its own shops, its own churches and its own social facilities. Many of our troops seldom mixed at all with the local population, so a lack of linguistic ability was hardly an issue. Most soldiers could manage 'Noch schwei bier bitte' (another two beers please) and by the end of the evening we all tended to become much more fluent so that the unfortunate vendors selling us bratwurst and chips on the way back to barracks from a night downtown had to endure a wonderful concoction of broken German spoken in a slurred broad Scottish accent. Fortunately, the menu choice was not very complex, and our money was good.

In those pre-euro days, we used the local currency, the Deutschmark, even in our own shops and facilities. We were paid through local German banks and so all had to open accounts. With the usual efficiency of an organisation that had been looking after troops in Germany for forty years, these bank accounts were arranged centrally through the army Pay Office. I have to say that we did feel somewhat superior to the US forces, who to us seemed even more insular than ourselves, to the extent of using US Dollars on their military bases in Germany (and I think in every other country they served in.). This meant that when we visited American bases, usually for the purpose of shopping at the PX (Post Exchange) where they had all sorts of goodies, like Weber barbeques at bargain prices, we had to change our German Deutschmarks into US Dollars.

As I prepared to move to BAOR for the first time in 1980, it quickly became evident to me that many members of the battalion had a good bit of previous experience of serving in Germany, and in fact a good number had been with KOSB when they were in Osnabruck in the early 1970s. The benefits of all this previous experience was diluted somewhat by all the 'experts' who were more than willing to share their own particular advice about what, and what not, to do. Their advice was not always useful.

We were posted to Osnabruck which for many years was the largest single British army garrison anywhere in the world outside Britain. The British population had peaked at about 12,000 troops. While this reduced over the years there were still 3,000 left for the final withdrawal parade on 13 June 2008. When we moved out there in 1980 there was the Brigade Headquarters, a Field Force eadquarters, three infantry battalions, a tank regiment and gunner regiment, lus all the supporting elements required to support these troops and their ependants.

There were, for example, three British Families Education Service primary chools. (During the early 1980s, BFES became the Service Children's ducation Authority (SCEA) and is now known as Service Children's ducation). These schools of course required staff. Teachers were given officer tatus, the married ones were accommodated in officers' married quarters on the atch, and the singles, who were mainly female, lived in the teachers' mess. The resence of a large number of single young women added greatly to the social fe of a largely male officer corps. I have lost count of the number of officers vho got married to SCEA teachers, despite the fact that commanding officers id not always approve.

One of the big challenges for me personally in moving to Germany was that had spent my first three years of military service based in the rather closeted tmosphere of the army in Scotland and, therefore, had seldom worked with haplains from other denominations. My working colleagues and senior haplains had all been Church of Scotland ministers. This changed when I rrived in Germany. There were five chaplains in the garrison – myself from the Church of Scotland, three Church of England and one Roman Catholic. The enior chaplain was Rev Tom Hiney MC, and the two other unit chaplains were Rev Colin Gibb and Rev Lesley Bryan.

Each of the other chaplains had his own church. The two main Anglican churches were large custom-built places of worship, both located in a barrack complex, one looked by Colin Gibb and the other by Lesley Bryan. Tom Hine led worship in St Luke's Garrison Church which was now run as an Anglican place of worship, but which had started off life as stable block. The KOSB had converted this building into their Regimental Kirk, Church of Scotland, during previous tour of duty in Osnabruck. On their departure from the garrison it had continued as a church with the form of worship being determined by the denomination of the individual chaplain looking after Belfast Barracks, situated across the road.

In the summer of 1980, KOSB moved into Quebec Barracks replacing one of the Parachute battalions. During their time in Osnabruck the Paras had converted a surplus wing of the cookhouse building into an extra gymnasium. Our quartermaster, with a little pressure from the Regimental Kirk Session, decided that this would be much better used by KOSB as the Regimental Kirk. After much borrowing and whatever else it is that QMs do to obtain blue carpet, blue curtains, 'chairs church' and various other important pieces of ecclesiastical furniture and fittings, a very lovely church was created. Our own regimental church accoutrements were added, and we were ready to open for worship.

The timing was perfect as the serving Moderator of the General Assembly of the Church of Scotland, The Rt Rev William B Johnston, was visiting troops in BAOR that summer, and it was arranged that he would come to dedicate our new Kirk. I prepared the Order of Service, received some input from the Moderator via his chaplain Rev Norman Drummond, who was serving as a regular army chaplain, padre of 1st Bn Black Watch at that time, and felt that we were pretty much 'good to go'. I knew Norman well. We had both studied at New College Edinburgh and had played rugby together. Both Norman and I came into the army without serving a Probationary Period in a civilian parish. I believe we were the only two ever allowed to do this.

Invitations had been sent to the other Church of Scotland army chaplains serving in Germany at the time, and everyone was keenly looking forward to the grand event. Padre Tom Hiney, my senior chaplain, called me up a week prior to the big day asking, "Stephen, could you confirm details for the part the DACG will play in the service next week?"

This took me a little by surprise. The deputy assistant chaplain general, Rev Graeme Roblin, was the divisional senior chaplain and an Anglican clergyman

I am not sure that I had met him yet, but he did seem pretty far removed from my sphere of influence and responsibility, and it had not even crossed my mind to involve him.

"But this is a Church of Scotland service," was my response. I was summoned to Tom's office where I was firmly put in the picture regarding the ecumenical nature of military chaplaincy, and the importance of the chaplaincy hierarchy. Both he and Rev Graeme Roblin, the deputy assistant chaplain general would attend, and the DACG would have a speaking part.

In the event the day was a great success. The sun shone, Christine baked a cake, the crowds turned up, and our church was well and truly dedicated. The latest evolution of the Regimental Kirk of the King's Own Scottish Borderers was complete and open for Sunday worship.

In his reflections on military life, Brigadier Frank Coutts, late KOSB, notes:

'Officers, for the most part, whether believers or not, looked on themselves as Regimental Christians and supported the Padre at voluntary church parades – services actually: they were not parades. They attended church and their wives particularly appreciated the opportunity to have their children attend Sunday School.'

Sunday worship was very much an officers' mess occasion. We did have a sprinkling of other ranks and their families who attended and blended in well and I don't think they felt excluded but I would guess that only those with a pretty strong commitment to Christ and his church would take the step of coming into barracks on a Sunday morning, a day off, to attend church with the Commanding Officer sitting in the front row. For the officers and their families church service was usually followed by drinks in the Mess, and often then by a curry lunch.

One sergeant explained to me that while he was a believer, and quite openly so, he wouldn't attend church on a Sunday. ""If they see me there, they'll ask me to read the lesson, so I'm staying away!"" Grown men, who would happily shout out commands on the parade square in front of 500 soldiers, are often intimidated when asked to read a Bible passage in church.

I did sympathise with all of this. As a minister of the Kirk I was used to writing my own prayers for Sunday worship with the knowledge that if I slipped up with my wording no one would know as no one else had a copy of the text. This, of course, is quite different when leading a Church of England service using the Book of Common Prayer, with everyone reading along in their own copy. I took me time to get used to covering Anglican services for my colleagues, learning the rhythm of the Prayer Book language, and not being distracted by the senior officer, kneeling a few feet from me. This mental discomfort was often multiplied by the physical pain of having to kneel at a prayer desk the morning after a game of rugby during which the opposing hooker had done his best kick my legs into a pulp. Leading worship standing up in the Kirk was so much easier.

We might not have got many of the ordinary soldiers to church on a Sunday, but they all came on a Thursday morning when we held Church Parade. This was an old tradition in many Scottish Regiments. It was a Commanding Officer's parade, and everyone attended.

It was a quick fifteen to twenty minutes with two hymns, a Bible reading, a brief sermon and a prayer. The men would form up in a hollow square, the Regimental Band would provide the music, and the Sergeant Majors would patrol behind the troops, prodding the mumblers in the ribs with their pace stick – "Sing up, man!"

It was a challenging weekly moment for any padre. You had to try and make sense, say something relevant, be spiritual without being too heavenly, and get off parade without having said anything that could be thrown back at you over coffee in the mess. There were times when current happenings in the unit would provide some material. On one occasion I came on to parade feeling very fed up that for the third time in two weeks different local German fathers had arrived in our barracks to complain about their daughters being made pregnant by our soldiers. I read something suitable from the Bible and then started my address, during which I got myself more and more wound up. I ended up saying something about them all behaving like rabbits and their brains hanging between their thighs. I stomped off the parade ground without offering a prayer or singing the second hymn. As I marched past the quartermaster, who was also my session clerk, he leaned towards me and said, "Feel better after that, Padre?"

Interestingly that is not the Church Muster people seem to remember. The one they do still talk about involved a bottle of whisky. A number of chaplains have repeated this, but I believe that it was Rev Stewart Hynd who first broke a bottle of whisky on the parade square in the middle of Church Muster. A large number of soldiers' free time activities do seem to include women and drink, and on this particular occasion Stewart was intent in making a point about the demon drink and the problem it was creating for the battalion. At the appropriate moment he held high his bottle of whisky, a bottle of Grouse which always seemed to be the most popular in army bars, ('though other brands are available', as they say) before smashing it on the ground in front of the 600 shocked soldiers and officers.

I am not sure it did any good, though it might well have convinced everybody that the padre was as daft as they already thought he was. *And what a waste of good whisky!* everybody thought. Years later someone told me that Stewart hadn't even paid for it but had presented a bill to the Regimental Fund. However, he did go down in history, and many another chaplain followed his example with a new generation of soldiers, and a fresh bottle of whisky. I always thought that I would have filled the bottle with cold tea rather than waste the amber nectar.

Sunday church services and church parades in Scottish infantry units were a great privilege for the chaplain and reflect something quite unique about church and chaplaincy in Jock units. Father Stephen Louden, goes some way to explaining this when he writes:

Research evidence provided by the Institute for American Church Growth, shows that churches grow, and grow best, where members have many characteristics in common and feel that they belong, by sharing similar interests and culture. In the context of the British army those chaplains who are the main

beneficiaries, supposing such factors to be operative, are Scottish Presbyteria
ministers when chaplain to Scottish regiments. The perception of belonging, i
such regiments, is given to both officers and soldiers by their shared nationa
and cultural background, strong regimental traditions and a heritage in whic
the regimental Kirk shares. The occasional attendance of a Scottish soldier a
the Kirk can provide a cohesive function not given by the attendance of a
equivalent English regimental soldier at a Church of England army church.

I served with Tom Hiney for two years and we got on pretty well. He wa
really my first brigade senior chaplain, and I think we both had to learn how thi
relationship best worked. On one occasion I returned home to Osnabruck havin
been away in Norway with the family on leave. We had driven the very lon
drive from Hirtshals on the northern tip of Denmark, with four children, and
wanted to collapse into bed for a good night's sleep before starting back to worl
the next day. I had in my mind a gentle first day back in the office working slowly
into the normal routine. So, I was pretty upset to find through the letter box o
our married quarter an A4 sheet of paper containing twenty-two points for actio
or response which Tom Hiney had left for my arrival.

Suitably annoyed, and dealing with tiredness and frustration, I sat down with
my own A4 sheet, wrote numbers 1 to 22 down the left border, and appended
one- or two-word responses to Tom's twenty-two points. I guessed that Tom had
just been adding to the list as points came into his mind during my weeks away
and that he would have no idea, for example, what point 15 was about and
therefore what my response 'will do that on Friday' could possibly refer to. I
sneaked down under the cover of darkness and posted my response list through
his front door, ready for him to find the following morning. Nothing was ever
said. And Tom never did leave another list.

While we were based in Osnabruck the Anglican Bishop to the Forces paid
an official visit. Tom, of course, was in charge, and he and his wife Muriel kindly
invited all the other chaplains and their families to their house for lunch. We
were dressed in Service Dress uniform with Sam Browne belt and No 1 Dress
hats. It was a lovely time enjoyed by everyone both young and old. It was the
next day that I realised that I had misplaced my good hat. After searching high
and low I remembered that the last place I had seen it was on arrival at Tom and
Muriel's quarter. It was a few weeks before my hat was discovered in the Hiney
children's dressing up box. Tom's son, also called Tom, in due course also

ecame an army chaplain. Looking back I realise that as a young lad looking up) his father with pride and respect and wanting to be like him when he grew up, e had taken advantage of my stray hat to pose and practise. He now has his own at!

In September 1980 we were involved in Exercise CRUSADER 80. This was he largest British peacetime exercise ever held on West German soil, and it sted the lines of communication and re-supply stretching right back to the United Kingdom and included the largest mobilisation of the territorial army. The scenario was based on a massive attack from the East, a threat which the British and American armoured formations had to face while based in Germany.

KOSB were providing umpires for the exercise (a bit like the person organising a paint ball battle at a stag party, but on a much grander scale!) and his meant that I was unable to accompany my own troops on the exercise. Tim Hiney was chaplain of the brigade headquarters which would take up all of his ime, so I was temporarily appointed a padre of 1st Battalion the King's Regiment or the two weeks. I spent the fortnight in a beech wood. It was a very relaxed ime visiting the various company locations, and I think the only negative aspect was on the last day. I was preparing to hold a church service in the field with all anks, when the officers all headed off to a local hostelry for a boozy lunch. My umour failed me, and I jumped into my Land Rover and headed back to Osnabruck. I have no idea if I was ever reported for cancelling the church service.

Life in BAOR was usually that oft spoken of combination of 'work hard, play hard'. We did work very hard at times, but we certainly played pretty hard as well. Much of our social life was centred on the mess, each level of the military ank structure having their own place to relax and socialise. The ready availability of duty-free drink played its part in ensuring that parties were well-oiled. This was not always good, and some of the behaviour which back then was accepted with humour would now be regarded with some concern.

There was limited interaction with the German community, though in all three of my postings in Germany some official efforts were made. Teaching us all Basic German helped a little, but at the end of a two-week course most of us could only greet people, ask how old they were and if they were married. I did sometimes wonder if basic German was really basic chat-up German. The next level up was the Colloquial German Course. It came with a financial reward for service personnel, and so was a little more attractive. Christine and I attended one of these courses together. I did learn a good bit more of the language, but I don't think Christine ever managed to make use of the German equivalent c 'Can I rent your barn for the night to keep my tank in it?'

We all quickly discovered that social events with our national hosts wer opportunities for them to perfect their English. Our stuttering and sometime highly embarrassing attempts to speak German were regarded with amusement

The relationship between British military personnel and the German civilia community were, in the Cold War days, always under the shadow of our concer about East German spies amongst the West German population. There was great sensitivity, and we were encouraged to be cautious.

I don't remember how many spies or sleepers the intelligence people told u that there were in West Germany, but it was surprisingly high. This meant tha we were to take care with whom we fraternised and how much information w shared. But how do you recognise a spy?

There was only one occasion when my suspicions were aroused sufficientl for me to feel that I ought to say something to the Royal Military Police. Quebe Barracks in Osnabruck was circled by a high barbed wire fence which at som places ran within a couple of metres of civilian houses and their gardens. Thes were at some distance from our actual buildings, but some local homes did permi the owners to see over our fence onto the sport fields from their upstair windows.

In one of those houses there lived a very friendly couple who had one son They attended the local Evangelische Kirche, and so were Protestants like mos of us. The man worked for DeutchePost and his wife was a schoolteacher. They both sang in the church choir, and they spoke remarkably good English. Ove some years they had built up friendly relationships with quite a number o members of the British military community, and quite soon after we settled i Osnabruck, I found myself inviting their church choir to attend and participate in one of our Regimental Kirk morning services.

It all seemed innocent enough until Christine and I were invited to their home for *Kaffee und Kuchen* (coffee and cake). They were lovely hosts, and we go talking to their 12-year-old boy who offered to show us the scale model o Quebec Barracks which his father and he had built in the cellar. (It is normal for German houses to have a fully functional set of rooms in the cellar, with the top third above ground level). It was a remarkably fine and accurate model.

I pondered this for some time. Here was a couple who had, when I though about it, good friendly relationships across the garrison, usually with just one person or a married couple in each unit: The chief clerk of the Kings Regiment, the chaplain of KOSB, and others elsewhere, and had a scale model of our barracks in their cellar. Anyway I passed the information on but never heard anything else about it.

The only time I thought about it again was when being force-marched past their house one day. We were en route to an overnight NBC (Nuclear Biological Chemical) training exercise. John Cooper was in charge and he had decided that it would be good for his soldiers to spend 24 hours wearing our NBC Kit complete with respirators. We marched out to the training area suitably dressed but with respirators off. On arrival a whistle blew, mess tins were banged together, people shouted out, "Gas, gas, gas", and we all struggled to get our respirators on and properly fitted. For the next 24 hours we undertook all sorts of tasks and challenges including communicating on the radio, eating, drinking and defecating (Yes, but most of us managed to avoid that bit) while fully protected against enemy attack.

After a less than peaceful night's sleep we were marched back the three miles into camp, still masked up. What a relief to arrive at last, and to hear the command, *"Unmask!"* I grabbed the bottom of my respirator, pulled it up over my face and almost threw up when a piece of my breakfast sausage fell out. It had been in there for three hours, rubbing against by cheek.

The rough times, and there were plenty of these as we did have a very serious function to fulfil as part of the military force prepared to confront any move by the Warsaw Pact countries into West Germany, were pretty well balanced by the good times which we enjoyed in a very full social life. In addition to the normal routine of parties and barbecues and dances, there were special occasions like the marriage of Prince Charles and Lady Diana Spencer in the summer of 1981. This provided a wonderful opportunity for street parties and celebrations, and for the KOSB this blended in well with our annual celebration of Minden Day on 1 August.

The smooth flow from one party onto the next quite often happened over the festive season. There were years when no one could take UK leave, and so the whole Battalion was in station, and available to be called out, not able to leave the garrison, but with not a lot of work to do. So, we were 'stood down' and free to celebrate Christmas and New Year. My memory is perhaps a little blurred but looking back it seems to me that in addition to some large mess activities there was on most days a lunch party in one house and then an evening dinner party somewhere else in the patch, and we all seemed to attend all of them.

We had one particular young officer who had got himself into trouble for enjoying himself too much on St Andrews Night and for his punishment the commanding officer had banned him from drinking over the festive season. This was a point of great rejoicing for all the other single living-in officers. They joined together and hired a large van for the ten days. Alastair was detailed as the driver, and the back was half filled with crates of beer. They would work out where the next party was being held and turn up *en masse*. The white van would arrive outside your front gate, the back door would open, and the subalterns would pour out, complete with beer, to join the party. When they had had enough they disappeared and headed off in search of more fun and probably younger and single, women.

Over the years since then the number of British troops in Germany has steadily been reduced. The 1993 Options for Change Defence Cuts resulted in BAOR dropping to about 25,000 strong, with a number of garrisons including Soest, Soltau and Minden closing.

Further repatriation of our troops has continued in recent decades and we are now left with around 185 British army personnel and 60 ministry of defence civilians permanently based at the 117-square kilometre Sennelager Training Area, near Paderborn, which provides both UK and NATO Forces with a live-firing training area. The facility allows for large-scale manoeuvres to be rehearsed and there is also an urban warfare training area.

I was speaking to one of my old CO's recently and talking about serving in Germany. We agreed that when the lamp starts swinging it tends to be party stories that get told rather than training and work ones. We did have an important task to fulfil, but thankfully in our time we never had to face enemy fire as part of the British Army of the Rhine.

Chapter 5

First Gulf War

"Live with the men, go everywhere they go... share their risks. Work in the very front and they will listen to you; but if you stay behind you are wasting your time." – Advice given by Rev Hardy VC DSO MC the most decorated of all wartime chaplains to Rev Studdert-Kennedy, 'Woodbine Willie'.

Life was to be quite different during my second posting to the British Army of the Rhine. In June 1989 I was sent to Werl as the padre of 1st Bn The Royal Scots, having failed to leave the army and been persuaded instead to complete a further four years so as to qualify for a service pension.

Christine and I had struggled with what we perceived to be God's plan for our life, and the fact that the chaplain general had a different understanding about where my future lay. We were coming to the end of a two-year posting in Berlin with the Black Watch and were sure that the next step for us was to leave the army and to go to the USA to work with the Vineyard Christian Fellowship. Leaving the army while based overseas wasn't quite as simple as we imagined, and it felt as though the chaplain general wasn't doing very much to make it any easier for us. At one point I even unplugged and hid the home telephone to make sure that Christine's threat to phone him personally was put on hold until we all calmed down a bit.

In the event I soldiered on and accepted the posting to 1 RS, and we moved to Werl in West Germany. We had already told the children that we were taking them out of boarding school, and so we went ahead with that and arranged to home-school them in our married quarter. This was a pretty novel concept in the military community, and I think the Royal Scots were a bit worried about what they were getting as their new chaplain. We were expecting to serve two years in Werl and then move with the battalion in an Arms Plot move back to Fort George in Inverness. The Arms Plot moved British army units around the world to ensure maximum flexibility and to give all units a good range of variety and experience. Having accepted my posting, and the plan for our next four years that came with it, we got on with life and soon settled into the familiar BAOR pattern of life that we had known and greatly enjoyed in Osnabruck eight years earlier.

For the first twelve months everything ran pretty smoothly but life changed dramatically in the summer of 1990 and by the November one of the biggest concerns for the families of the Royal Scots serving in Germany was when they should celebrate Christmas. The men were preparing to deploy to the Gulf, most of them departing before Christmas and none of them with any idea how long they would be gone. So, when would Santa come with presents for the children? And will the NAAFI be able to supply sufficient turkeys if lots of people decide to celebrate early? Some celebrated with Dad before the men deployed, others went ahead on 25 December without him, and a few decided to wait until he returned and have a full turkey dinner in the spring complete with Christmas trees, tinsel and presents.

It was really only a problem for the married men and their families. The single men based in the barracks had most of the decisions made for them. The officers' mess and the warrant officers and sergeants' mess had been closed down and everyone was eating in the soldiers' cookhouse. There would be no egimental Christmas parties, though the officers, dressed in olive denims, did manage to celebrate St Andrews Day with a regimental dinner but with no silver in the table. It was some months before we realised just how much our lives had een changed by events East of Suez, when on 2 August 1990 Iraqi forces invaded Kuwait and on the 28th Saddam Hussein declared Kuwait to be the 19th province of Iraq.

Over the coming weeks there were lots of rumours and counter-rumours about how the rest of the world would respond to these events, and how the British army might be involved. The end of the Cold War meant that there was less necessity to keep our troops in West Germany and the feeling grew that surely if British troops were to take part in any operation, then most of them would come from Germany-based units. Desert warfare would require main battle tanks and most of ours were sitting on the North German plain. Here was an opportunity to use them for what they were built, and with the Royal Scots being armoured infantry with warrior fighting vehicles, surely any plan would include the Royal Scots.

I struggled a bit at first with what felt like warmongering. My focus was on preparing for civvy life and the last thing I wanted to do was go to war, so I was pleased when the opportunity came for me and the family to return to the UK on leave. I actually spent a fair bit of my three weeks' leave attending two Vineyard Christian Fellowship conferences. This was the church organisation that I was hoping to work with when I eventually escaped from the RAChD and I was keen to connect again with the leader, John Wimber, and secure his blessing for my future plans.

During this time I kept one eye on the news and on information coming back from the Royal Scots. The story seemed to keep changing. Initially the Royal were not going to deploy to the Gulf on Operation GRANBY (The British military contribution to the international coalition that was being built to confront Saddam Hussein) but would be used to protect German ports through which supplies of 7th brigade were being shipped out to the Gulf. This really upset lot of soldiers. There is nothing worse than standing on the quayside waving you comrades off to war, especially when you reckon you could do a better job yourself.

The next version of the story was that the battalion would be part of Op GRANBY 2 as part of 4 Brigade which would replace 7 Brigade in April 1991 This was regarded as not ideal but better than nothing but carried the danger tha the fighting might be over by the time we got out there. And then on 1 November the news came through that we were to deploy within weeks as par of Operation GRANBY 1.5 which was to provide a further armoured brigade to complete the 1st (British) Armoured Division in Saudi Arabia.

We had just a few weeks to prepare to go to war, and there was no time to hang around. Life took on a strange sense of unreality. Winter was slowly settling in, and here we were based in a small town in Germany and planning to deploy to the Gulf to fight an enemy who had a terrible reputation for using unpleasant and illegal means to get his own way. Everything had to change. The daily routine, the level of fitness, the focus of life. It seemed that every aspect of our existence had to be reconsidered. On a personal level wills had to be written insurances taken out, and domestic banking arrangements sorted out.

The officers' mess was packed up and closed down. It was assumed correctly in the event, that we would go and sort out Saddam Hussein, and then move as a unit back to Scotland, and so while we prepared our kit and equipment to go to war, at the same time we packed up everything that was to be left behind ready for the removal of the whole unit to inverness.

A new daily programme was developed with the whole battalion mustering in the gymnasium at 06:00 hours. Every day started with a Bible reading and a hought for the day from the Padre followed by a prayer. This was an enormous privilege, but I was very aware that I mustn't ruin this daily opportunity. Soldiers don't suffer fools gladly, and if I just got up and waffled every morning then I would lose the confidence of the men and be less able to minister to them in the middle of the war which we were preparing to fight.

We had given each man a New Testament with a reading plan at the back. This gave a short passage to be read each day. I decided that by way of trying to encourage daily Bible reading that I should use this reading plan at the daily muster parades. I had not, however, reckoned with the fact that it was now into December and we had reached the book of Revelation with all its dramatic end times material. This made for some interesting morning readings.

Lt Colonel Iain Johnston, our commanding officer, was hugely supportive of my ministry. He was a man of faith and was keen to see his men well supported spiritually. One afternoon I was summoned to his office. I was a wee bit surprised to see the regimental sergeant major accompany me as I marched in and saluted the boss sitting behind 'the big tartan table'. The CO explained that he wanted every soldier to have at least two prayers that he could say on his own, i.e., the Lord's Prayer and the regimental collect.

Each unit in the army has its own prayer, and the regimental collect of the Royal Scots (The Royal Regiment) is:

O Lord Jesus Christ, Who art the first and the last, grant we pray Thee, that, as Thou hast promised to be with us even unto the end of the world, so may the Royal Scots be the first to follow Thee and the last to forsake Thee, who art with the Father and the Holy Ghost, one God, world without end. Amen.

It is a really rousing prayer and very appropriate for warfighting situations.

"I want every soldier to learn the collect, so he can pray it on his own and we can pray it together at church services." I was surprised and very grateful for the support, but not at all sure that this was achievable.

"So, ehm, how will we make that happen, sir?"

"Nae problem, Padre!" interjected the RSM. "I'll get that sorted out right away." And he did.

The Collect was included in that day's Part One Orders, the daily orders which everyone reads carefully and which lays out the duties and events for the following day. Everyone was given 48 hours to learn the prayer and thereafter no one was allowed out of camp without reciting it to whoever was on guard Not being able to leave camp meant that the married men couldn't go home to their wives and families, and that the single men couldn't go out to do whatever it is that single soldiers find to do on their time off.

Within a couple of days you could hear the regimental collect being recited by squads running through the woods, similar to American soldiers running along to their marching songs. And there was a lot of running through the woods The physical preparation was challenging. I remember spending the occasional PT period in the sauna, where we took turns to ride the fitness bike that had been placed there. Outside was early winter with snow on the ground, inside the sauna was more like what we expected out in the Gulf.

It was a busy and disorientating few weeks. Alongside all the battalion preparations there was a lot of personal matters to deal with. At work I was issued with a Land Rover and told that I needed to work out what to load it with. I scrounged a wood and metal box, about the size of my children's boarding school trunks, painted it the sandy colour that everything else was being painted in, and transformed it into my battle box. After some care thought I packed the battle box with a collection of Bibles, hymnbooks and reading material.

I was also 'issued' with my driver. There weren't any spare drivers within the battalion, so Private Butcher from 1st Battalion the Queen's Own Highlanders was allocated to me. We were an unusual pair, but we got on extremely well. I think it was all a bit of a shock for 'Butch' to start with. Soldiers never like the idea of being posted to another unit, because there is no unit quite as good as their own. Perhaps the opportunity to go to war helped him accept the command to report to the Royal Scots with at least some enthusiasm but hearing on arrival that his task was to be the padre's driver might well have diluted even that. He was, however, ideal for the task.

Things changed for the family as well. Christine and I decided to bring the home schooling to an end. Our oldest girl, Barbara, had already taken herself off to the local German High School or Gymnasium. Malcolm decided to join her there, and the younger two started attending the army primary school with all the other Royal Scot children.

Christine found herself being expected to play a more prominent role among the families, and alongside the other officers' wives received briefing in grief and bereavement counselling. The men were going to war. They were not all xpected to make it home. The officers' wives would be expected to become welfare workers for the other ranks' dependents.

In the midst of this increasingly gloomy setting I came home one lunchtime o be greeted by Christine looking cheerier than normal. "I've been reading 'salm 91 this morning, and I believe it is a promise for us that you will come come safely." I read through the passage and it certainly is a very positive and comforting Psalm. "Well, it would be lovely if that really was a word for us," I numbled, "but I think I would need more proof to put any faith in it." It wasn't he response Christine was hoping for, but my view changed the next day when opened my mail.

Some years back, in Hong Kong with the Scots Guards, I had dedicated the on of one of our corporals. We had started off discussing a service of baptism or the baby, but it quickly became evident that the parents didn't believe in God at all, never mind having any Christian commitment. They were happy, however, o go ahead with a service of dedication and all was well. The letter I had just received was from this corporal. He had left the army and the family had settled n Aberdeen. Our conversation about God and baptism has stirred them to explore the Christian faith and they were now writing to me to let me know that they had both accepted Jesus Christ as their Lord and Saviour, and also to say that they knew I was preparing to go to war with the Royal Scots and they believed that Psalm 91 was a promise of safety for me in the battle ahead. I was surprised to say the least.

After another friend spoke to me about Psalm 91, completely out of the blue, I started to believe in Christine's interpretation of the Psalm. We talked it all through with the children and decided that it would be good to find out if my friend Ian White had written new music for this particular Psalm. Ian had published a couple of albums of some of the Psalms in a modern idiom. Our ten-year-old daughter Caroline was tasked with writing to Ian to explain the whole story and to ask if he had recorded a version. Within a week the reply arrived. Although he had written the words and composed the music, he had not previously got round to recording Psalm 91. But he had now, and he sent a cassette copy to Caroline. Over the coming months the children made many copies which were distributed among the soldiers of the Royal Scots.

It was now well through December and the families who were celebrating Christmas early had done so, and their men were on their way to the Gulf. I had been instructed to stay behind in Germany to spend Christmas with the families and the rear party, and so I was in the last group of Royal Scots to fly out to the Middle East. At 08:00 hours on Boxing Day 1990 I reported to the barracks in Werl, West Germany and boarded the bus that would take us on the first stage of our journey to war. Most of the battalion was already out in Saudi Arabia. We all experienced a strange mixture of emotions as the bus turned out of the familiar barrack gates and took us off into an unknown future. We were off to war.

* * * * *

My home for the first few days after we arrived in theatre was Blackadder Camp in Al Jubail in north east Saudi Arabia. The camp had featured in BBC TV news reports that I had seen on British Forces Broadcasting Service (BFBS) television back in Germany, so the sight didn't surprise me. Long rows of brown accommodation tents set out with military precision, a huge amount of activity, centralised eating arrangements, primitive ablutions and rows of blue Porta-loos. I read somewhere that a senior officer's daughter named the camp. It does seem strange now that many years later I was minister of a parish in Berwickshire which contained the ruins of Blackadder House and through which flowed the Blackadder tributary of the River Tweed.

Most people hated being in that camp and longed to escape out into the open spaces of the training areas in the desert where we could shake out and be on our own. But for me Blackadder Camp held a strange attraction. I had spent most of my teenage summer holidays at Christian summer camps run by Scripture Union at a campsite called Scoughall between Dunbar and North Berwick in East Lothian. My great uncle Rev Jim Meiklejohn MBE, known as 'Boss' to generations of SU campers, had played a leading role in the creation of these camps which were initially called Inter School Camps (ISC). It was a bit of a family business. (Looking back now it is amusing to remember that we also ran a parallel set of camps for the posh kids who went to private school. Varsity and Public School (VPS) camps had their own staff but the same evangelical ethos.) At Scoughall we slept in tents pitched on sandy soil, and it was there that I experienced much of my early spiritual moments. For me the smell of sand and canvas was connected with God and spiritual contentment. Smell has a powerful effect on our minds. Most of us love the smell of fresh bread and know how it makes our mouths water. Supermarket designers are skilled in using this sensory response to encourage customers to buy from the bakery shelves. When I arrived

Blackadder Camp, the smell of sand and canvas felt very familiar, my brain icked in and I was very much at home.

I was to spend a week or so based in Blackadder. I met up with my driver Butch (Private Butcher) and our Land Rover, though within a few days it was taken from us, apparently required for more urgent operational training purposes. The Brigade senior chaplain came to welcome me and to brief me on what he expected of me. The best thing he achieved was obtaining a Toyota Land Cruiser to replace the Land Rover that our Operations Officer, Captain Neil Brownlie, had removed from me. (I never did let Neil forget that he had done this – so, Neil, if you are reading this!)

Butch and I were thrilled with our brand-new vehicle. Boys and their toys. We got some red cross and red crescent stickers to identify us as non-combatants, had a roof rack fitted to carry all our kit, and then we argued at the start of every trip about who was going to drive. Butch quite rightly tried to point out that he was the 'padre's driver' and that this was HIS vehicle. From my side I tried suggesting that as with US army chaplains' assistants (a special corps within the US army), he was the one who was armed and so perhaps he should be sitting in the passenger seat, wide-eyed and alert, ready to defend the padre. Most of the time we took turns. We did love that vehicle!

In the end we actually only had it for a couple of weeks. It had been allocated to one of the field hospital chaplains who was due in theatre, and on his arrival the brigade senior chaplain searched me out with a replacement, somewhat beaten up, old Land Rover. I was out in the desert by this time and managed to avoid him for a few days, but he was pretty persistent and was sitting waiting for me one evening at our Battalion Headquarters. With great sadness we unpacked our beloved Land Cruiser and handed over the keys. The replacement tatty old Land Rover did nothing for my image!

Anyway, back to Blackadder...

I used the days there to connect with other chaplains, find the NAAFI HQ, obtain maps and to scrounge any other pieces of equipment that Butch and I thought might come in handy. The maps were of only minimal benefit. Lots of yellow open countryside and a few roads. The maps were fine until you went 'off road'.

Philip Mayer, who was padre of Royal Scots Dragoon Guards and had been in theatre of operations for some months by this time, took me out for afternoon tea in a very smart hotel. He was serving with the cavalry and had been in Saudi for a few months, so he was full of good stories and wisdom, and had lots of useful connections which came from serving with the 'Cav'. There is a saying 'If you ain't, Cav, you ain't,' and they did very often seem to have a touch of glamour that opened doors which remained firmly closed to us mere mortals.

I held my first church service in Saudi Arabia in Blackadder Camp. We chose a location out of sight of the local population because what we were doing was probably illegal in the eyes of the Saudi Government – holding a Christian service in a public place.

Before deploying out to the Gulf there had been many reports about the challenges of serving in such a strictly Moslem country and the ways in which the Americans had adapted their practices. One suggestion was that US women drivers would not be allowed to drive, and it was also reported that the American chaplains would remove the Christian crosses from their uniform collars and that they would be referred to as 'welfare workers'. Would we take a similar approach? The answer from the chaplain general Jim Harkness was a very clear "No!" If the powers-that-be wanted British army chaplains on the operation, then we would go as chaplains. (See Appendix D for the formal instruction which was issued)

And then, of course, there was the question of Communion Wine. Alcohol was pretty much banned in Saudi Arabia. What were we going to use for the Sacrament? I now minister in a church where we offer fruit juice as an alternative to wine for Holy Communion, so as to avoid difficulties for those who have a problem – of addiction or conviction – to the drinking of alcohol. But while serving in the army we used a good quality Port. Or perhaps that was just in Scottish regiments.

After I left the regular army, I introduced port for Holy Communion in my first parish. When I went there, they were using a pretty nasty South African Sherry from the local Spar shop. After a couple of Communion Seasons (we celebrated the Lord's Supper four times a year), I persuaded the session clerk that we should try using port for the Common Cup (chalice) used by the Elders sitting around the Communion Table. The session clerk enjoyed his sip of port so much he suggested we introduce it for the whole congregation.

The change was wonderful! Firstly, because it stopped everyone coughing on the rough sherry and instead we soothed their throats with a nice sip of port (those in the know will be aware of the importance to drill sergeants of a glass of port for soothing the throat before taking spring drills), and secondly because of the wonderful odour that filled the church building as a result of 150 individual glasses of port having sat out all Saturday night with the heating on, ready and waiting for the Sunday morning Communion Service.

Anyway, we still had to make a decision. I do recall the brigade chaplains' meeting in Munster where the topic was discussed, but I am not at all sure what was decided. I, however, did decide what to do and I carefully wrapped up three bottles of port of an acceptable quality (from the officers' mess) and packed them away in my battle box, along with a supply of Church of Scotland Field Service Books, my communion kit, and a Royal Stewart Piper's Plaid (inherited from Padre John Murdoch who left it behind in Hong Kong some years previously) a few Bibles and other odds and ends. The battle box was transferred to the Padre's Land Rover along with a picnic table I had bought in East Berlin which I would use as an altar. These bottles of port never did make it onto that Communion Table.

I was still in Blackadder Camp on Hogmanay. There wasn't much to do. I was sitting reading in my tent when a couple of Royal Scot senior ranks appeared. After some idle chat, that didn't seem to be going anywhere in particular, the topic of Communion Wine came up. "Come on, Padre, it's Hogmanay. Surely you could spare us a bottle or two?" This conversation continued off and on at various times throughout the evening. They were clearly making a concerted effort and I was probably a bit of a soft touch. Once they had managed to get out of me that I did actually have three bottles of port, they then started on the argument that it would be detrimental to the morale of the troops if only those taking Holy Communion were given access to alcohol during the forthcoming military action. In fact, I could end up with soldiers coming to Communion just for 'a wee slug of booze!'

Little did I know that my eventual surrender, enjoyable though it was (because I too enjoyed a little port that evening), would appear in the national press two days later.

THE INDEPENDENT newspaper included an article titled **A Toast to Scotland the Brave in 'liberated' Communion wine.** Charles Richards wrote:

It was a cruel Hogmanay for the 1st Battalion, the Royal Scots. The advance party who arrived up to three weeks ago had to make do with British Legion food parcels of 'Irn Bru' and shortcake – although one sergeant-major bragged that he had liberated three bottles of Communion wine from the Padre. We tried to pretend it was a 12-year-old malt but it didn't work.

I never did find out which senior rank had 'bubbled me' and thankfully never heard how the chaplain general responded when he heard of our Hogmanay celebrations in Blackadder Camp. As we approached 'the bells' at midnight marking the start of 1991, the troops had appeared from their tents with the means to 'see in' the New Year. The Sunday Post newspaper had sent every Scot in the Gulf a small box of typical Scottish goodies: A can of Irn Bru (Scotland's other national drink – made in Scotland from girders!) some shortbread, an Oor Wullie comic and I think some Black Bun.

We gathered in the dark, with the glow of the nearby streetlamps casting some light into the camp causing lots of shadows. There were some miniatures of whisky that had been secreted illegally in amongst individual's army kit for the journey out to the Gulf. We listened to the bells on the radio, a piper played, toasts were shared, small eats devoured, and then an eerie silence fell as we started to make our individual ways back to our beds. A New Year had arrived, but what on earth this year would hold for us, we had no idea. There was a lot to think about and not many words to express any of it. Silence seemed the only answer, and in silence we started 1991, the year we would go to war; many of us for the first and only time.

It was the reporter Richard Kay who gave me the nickname 'Arthur Daley of the Desert'. He reckoned that I was *'a man who could prosper from any exchange and as skilled a negotiator as the company quartermaster'*.

I think he was really quite a long way from the truth, and in fact Butch was probably much nearer to Arthur Daley in character and skill. Together we did do a lot of negotiating and selling, and more often than not we seemed to prosper. Butch, who did have a somewhat shifty look about him, would sometimes go off on his own and return with some amazing new supplies, often having sweet-talked some Americans who always seemed to have more kit than they knew what to do with, and were pretty easy bartering material, especially when it came to a Glengarry bunnet.

Jocks have always had the good fortune of 'owning' bits of tartan uniform. In 1979, when driving out of the front gate of Fort Campbell, Kentucky USA, I noticed a pair of Leslie Tartan trews for sale in the window of the pawn shop located right across the road camp. I was on Exercise TRUMPET DANCE with st Bn Kings Own Scottish Borderers. Of course, the Jock who had used his tartan rews to raise cash didn't actually own the trousers and would have to pay the price, not only of the lost kit but also perhaps for the misbehaviour. But, hey, here are times when the instant solution seems the best!

On Op GRANBY, in the Gulf, it was Glengarries rather than trews that we had available to swap, and the Americans were suckers for them. Butch could get a few American cot beds in exchange for each one. The cot beds – camp beds o us – were a great asset. We were travelling light and very few of us had our own British army issue camp beds, so getting your hands on one of these superior beds was a real joy. I still have mine nearly thirty years later.

Butch also did a lot of swopping of rations. Although we were issued a good supply of fresh supplements such as bread and eggs to enhance the basic rations, we lived largely off our own British army 'Compo' ration packs, and these did quickly become pretty boring. They had, of course, been the same since the Boer War – well, for a long time anyway!

The US army had MREs – Meals Ready to Eat. They contained all sorts of wonderful goodies which after a time became as boring as our own rations, but change is always good. Some menus had bread packed in airtight foil with a 'best before date' four or five years into the future. You do wonder how much good the contents did you. But whatever the nutritional value, the best thing was that the hot meals were 'boil in the bag' – a concept which had yet to hit the Ministry of Defence. These could be heated up 'on the move' in the BV ('Boiling Vessel' I imagine) inside the Warrior. There was always a market for them and Butch and I maintained our popularity by keeping the supply lines open.

We also kept up morale by running a shop out of the back of our Land Rover. It all began with a request for some cigarettes, but quickly developed to adapt to the new situation we all found ourselves in.

On army exercises back home, it was traditionally the 'Q Bloke', the company quartermaster sergeant, who supplied the cigarettes and chocolate bars and drinks. He would run a wee shop from the back of his truck as a side-line to his other duties as he moved about the exercise area delivering various supplies such as ammunition and rations to the troops on the ground. But that was on exercise, when there was less pressure and more time, and it only lasted a few days or a couple of weeks. Here, it was serious stuff, lasting week after week, and the Q bloke was more concerned about making sure that vital supplies of rations, water, and ammunition and other important equipment were always

delivered to the troops as promptly and efficiently as possible. He had no time t
go wandering back to Al Jubail for the extra luxuries the jocks were asking for

It started with the lads running out of cigarettes or fancying a can of Coke o
a chocolate bar. I would take a note of what they wanted and promise to retur
in a day or two with their order, but it all got a bit complex and pretty soon Butc
and I would just buy up whatever we could find in the local shop and sell it or
One of our favourite locations was a garage on the route from Al Jubail to Basra
We would go in there with whatever money was in our fund, spend it all o
everything we thought the guys would like and then head back and open up sho
at each company location. Pretty soon our range included cigarettes, drinks
sweets, batteries, electric razors and radios. Ah yes, and Goober Grape, which i
described by the manufacturer as *the ultimate combo made wit*
Smucker's Grape Jelly. Perfect for that classic peanut butter and jell
sandwich.' Basically it is peanut butter and jelly in a jar. It was very popular.

As days drifted into weeks, the requests became more complex. Birthday
and anniversaries started to creep up on us. "Hey, Padre, how am I going to sen
flowers to my missus on her birthday?" Good question! How do you send flower
home to your wife on your wedding anniversary when you are in the middle o
the desert? Easy! Just use Interflora. And it would have been easy if everyon
who wanted to order flowers could get themselves to the NAAFI base in A
Jubail. It was much more difficult when you try to do it through an intermediary
So the solution was for me to become an Interflora agent myself. I had a cha
with NAAFI, got my own Agency number, designed a simplified order form fo
use out in the locations, and I was up and running. We sent home hundreds o
flower orders.

The days were moving on and 14 February was just over the horizon. On on
of my weekly trips down to the NAAFI in Al Jubail I noticed that they ha
Valentine Cards in stock. I bought 400 of them and took them round the troops
We had a lot of married men with wives and families left behind in Germany. I
explained that if they bought a card from me there and then, wrote their loving
messages inside and addressed the envelope before I left their location, that I
would arrange for delivery of the card on 14 February.

The BFPO (British Forces Post Office) mail system in Germany required you
to collect your personal post from the Post Bunk. There was no postie coming
round the married quarters estate. You had to go and check for yourself each day.
I arranged for all 400 cards to be sent back to Germany as official mail and then

74

anded in to the Post Bunk ready for Valentine's Day itself. It was a great success xcept perhaps for those wives who didn't get one. I am sure there were some retty fed-up wives that day, but there were also hundreds of happy wives and ots of soldiers who had done the romantic thing thousands of miles from home.

Every war provides an opportunity to make money and even the makers of uddly toys cashed in. They designed teddy bears dressed in desert combats wearing a Tam O' Shanter hat. They even managed to put a Hunting Stewart artan (Royal Scots tartan) patch on the TOS (though the stripe wasn't always ngled properly – bloody civvies!). They could only be ordered by post but the only way of paying was by Postal Order and the only way of buying these was t the Field Post Office.

One day, just before we moved much further towards the border with Iraq, Butch and I set off for the Field Post Office with £2,000 of Saudi riyals (or Madrids' as the Jocks called them… from Real Madrid FC!). "I need £2,000 worth of postal orders please," I announced with a certain amount of pride. Unfortunately, the highest denomination they had was twenty pounds. I had to buy 120 in all, and each with a stampage fee. So much for everyone making money from war.

But the cards, the flowers and the teddy bears all got through, and the morale of the jocks was kept high as we prepared for action.

An important part of the padre's role is talking, well, listening more than alking. Being available for the men to offload on, or to confide in, or to confess o. Someone outside the strict chain of command who will listen and keep things confidential. 'It's good to talk!' and it is good for soldiers to talk, especially when hey are under the pressure of facing an enemy who might well use chemical weapons against them. Far from home, before mobile phones (though I do seem to remember that one of the Cavalry officers had his own personal satellite phone) with no access to any communication except letters. And then sometimes the longed-for letters would contain difficult or tragic news.

On a few very rare occasions, and always very much 'life and death', I was able to arrange for individuals to phone back to UK or Germany through the military communication system. This always required authority from Brigade and usually involved a lot of waiting for the correct connections and access to be made. The soldiers involved always benefitted from these brief live conversations with their loved ones.

I knew that I had to make myself as available as possible to the troops. needed to be there when they wanted to talk. It was important to make it as eas as possible for them to raise their concerns and I worked hard to minimise th barriers caused by me being an officer and a clergyman. By becoming shopkeeper, an Interflora agent, the distributer of soft toilet paper, a source c the little comforts of life, I put myself in a position where it was easy for peopl to approach me for a chat. Often a soldier would come to the shop set u alongside my Land Rover. In the middle of stocking up on supplies he woul say, "Padre, can I have a wee chat?" and at an opportune moment I would han over the running of the shop to Butch, and the soldier and I would find som privacy to talk about whatever was on his mind.

Often it was something as simple, but as important, as wanting to give m his 'final letter' which was to be locked away and only handed over to his wif partner or parents on the event of his death. I had quite a number of these in m safe-keeping and was always humbled that the men would trust me with suc precious items. In later conflicts an improved system was developed to make th writing and securing of these 'final letters' more official, but this wasn't ye available during Op GRANBY and so the padre filled this gap.

Other times we talked about life and death, children, hope and fears. Man of them have drifted together in my memory but one or two stand out. There wa one day when a corporal came to me and said that he wanted me to read a lette he had just received from his wife. I wondered if he was having problems readin it, but no, he had fully understood it all, and wanted me to read it as well. I trie to suggest that I really did not want to read his private mail, but he insisted, so gave in.

His wife told of an unusual experience she had had a week or so ago. Sh was lying in the bath thinking about things and the men being away in the Gul and praying to God that he would keep her husband safe. Suddenly, (I gues these things are always sudden) Jesus was standing at the bottom of the bath. Sh got such a fright, she jumped out of the bath and lit a cigarette to calm her nerves and only then she remembered to cover herself up! And the reason why I had to read this was that she then went on to instruct her husband to go and see the padre and become a Christian before the hostilities started for real.

And so we sat on the tail gate of my Land Rover and discussed what it mean to be a Christian and we prayed together. He picked up his purchases from the padre's shop and went back to his Warrior vehicle relieved that he had done the right thing for his wife and hopefully also for him.

The shop was a great success. We didn't make any money, but we did supply lots of needs and provide some extra comforts, and I found myself talking freely with many of my parish who might otherwise have found it difficult to approach me. And there was really only one time that our commercial activities almost got Butch and me into trouble, but more of that later.

Chapter 6
Church in the Desert

"I pray that we would let God take us through the desert – not just so that we can arrive in the Promised Land, but so that we can talk, or simply listen, to Him along the way." – Katie Kiesler, Because I Love You

Our church service in Blackadder Camp at the end of December 1990 had been quite a small affair with only 40 of us present. The rest of the battalion had already deployed further north into the desert to continue training for the conflict ahead. The wide-open countryside would allow the commanding officer to ensure that all the skills required for desert warfare were finely honed as we built up to what Saddam Hussein had promised us would be the 'mother of all battles'.

n the midst of a hugely busy training programme I had to find my place and an
nportant part of that was conducting church services.

Like a number of other Scottish infantry battalions, the Royal Scots still
aintained the tradition of Church Muster. This was a commanding officer's
arade and so everyone attended, believers and non-believers, Protestants and
oman Catholics, we came together and benefitted from the strength of common
lentity and a shared sense of unity. Church Muster usually consisted of two
ymns with a Bible reading, a short sermon and a prayer (and, of course, the
egimental collect) with the passage of Scripture usually being read by the
ommanding officer. The spiritual welfare of the men was important, and I had
part to play in ensuring their overall wellbeing.

There was of course always the option of non-attendance for those who
bjected to being forced to be part of a church service, but in my experience very
ew ever exercised this option. Perhaps the realisation that the RSM would find
omething else to keep such individuals occupied during the service, and concern
bout what exactly that might involve, encouraged a quiet acceptance. During
ny time in Elizabeth Barracks, Pirbright, I remember young recruits at the
Guards Depot being sent out to sweep up leaves on a wet and windy October
Sunday morning. The following week they opted to attend the church service.
The sermon might be boring but at least it was dry and warm inside the kirk.

Some army life was about the survival of the fittest, but quite a lot of it was
bout the survival of the quietest, the ones who just kept their head down and
lidn't attract unnecessary attention.

Over the next 3 months in early 1991 church services became a regular
eature of our life in the desert. They presented an opportunity not just for
orporate worship but also for strengthening our identity and interdependence as
a battle group. We were all in this together and seeing everyone else 'on parade'
was important. Very few members of the battalion were able to move freely
around the other companies as most were working in their own small team,
linked to the other subunits but physically separated from them. Seeing your
mates, many of whom had served together for 15 or 20 years, was good for
morale.

Most weeks I conducted individual company services, but from time to time
the CO would pull together the whole battlegroup. By this time all our various
additional elements had arrived and were under command. These included a
squadron of tanks, extra medics and mechanics, and Queen's Company of the

Grenadier Guards. For battlegroup church services we would form a hollow square, with the grenadiers forming one side. The Guards usually waited until everyone else was formed up, and then they would come thundering across the desert to join us, marching as if they were trooping the colour on Horseguards Parade. As they arrived on parade and the company sergeant major called 'Halt' they would put their feet in, and a cloud of dust would rise in the silence. And it would be time to start church. Their height and the drill added some gravitas to the occasion.

Other chaplains were of course conducting church services throughout the two brigades, but none of this was being reported back at home. The concern about upsetting our Saudi hosts had resulted in the Foreign and Commonwealth Office enforcing a press embargo on the reporting of Christian activity while we were in Saudi Arabia. No one wanted to upset our host country. Christian worship was illegal.

The result was that back in the UK there was no press reporting on the work of army chaplains and no mention of church. This upset many of the folk who were concerned about our welfare and were praying for our safety. Voices began to be raised. Where are the chaplains? Who is caring for the spiritual welfare of the troops?

That was all to change on Saturday, 2 February.

On Thursday, 31 January, Butch and I were doing the rounds of the company locations. I had been delegated the responsibility of distributing the incoming personal mail from UK and elsewhere, which came to us through the British Forces Post Office (BFPO) service. We were also receiving hundreds of welfare parcels sent out to the troops by the general public. These parcels were a huge encouragement to the soldiers and were always very welcome, and I had the joy of handing them out to the men. It was a bit like Christmas every day, and the padre was Santa! In addition to the letters and parcels that day I had been asked to distribute hundreds of rolls of soft toilet paper which the Quartermaster had managed to obtain from some source he wasn't willing to divulge. You have no idea how welcome a roll of soft toilet paper can be when you have used scratchy stuff for a few weeks. I was very popular.

When we arrived at B Company Richard Kay and Mike Moore, our embedded reporter and press photographer, met me. They had discussed with Major John Potter the possibility of submitting a report on a Royal Scots church service. John had apparently been his usual blunt self; "If they want us here to defend their country then they are going to have to put up with our customs. We are not going to hide church away from you guys." I was less worried about upsetting the locals – there weren't any anywhere near us at that time – but I did suggest that the censors back in the Foreign and Commonwealth Office would block any report; "But please feel free to take photos and submit a report. Who knows?"

And so Richard Kay sent the following dispatch to the Daily Mail:

The Padre bounced across the desert in a Land Rover stripped down for warfare. He had taken a four-pound hammer to the windscreen and all the other glass, and had etched the word chaplain' on the bonnet. Sporting a traditional shemagh headdress, Stephen Blakey jumped into the sand with all the enthusiasm of a sergeant-major about to lead his men into battle. But the men who gathered at his feet had come looking for spiritual guidance to carry with them on the eve of conflict. He told them that they had been sent by mankind to put right an evil – but that could not be achieved without a cost. He was saying that while it would be nice if, for the task ahead, we prayed that God would put a shield around us – a sort of thickened body armour if you like – He did not deal in insurance policies.

The Padre's delivery, in the plain, blunt language of the Royal Scots who faced him, boomed across the sand. This was a man of God who could see good in the right to wage war. When I looked into the young faces rubbed raw by the wind and sun, I swear I could see a kind of contentment settle over them as they prayed. We were sitting cross-legged on the ground or on bunched-up packs of webbing, and we clasped the blue order-of-service books of the Church of Scotland. As a concession to the moment we discarded our helmets, but the weapons of war lay at our feet. There were 165 soldiers, B Company's finest. Young men of extraordinary contradictions with their cropped heads, tattooed biceps and dark glasses, their language coarse and studded with profanities but their boots polished to a parade ground shine for their appointment with the padre.

From the moment the opening bars of Highland Cathedral floated across our heads there was a growing anticipation. This was probably the last time Bravo Company would assemble for church before they were committed to battle. The Padre had put up a trestle table, covering it with tartan and crisp white linen. From a travelling kit of sacraments he brought out a simple wooden cross and a

81

silver Communion cup. For bread he broke pieces of brown biscuit from a comp
ration box. Unaccompanied by music, men sang Fight the Good Fight, a hymn
that could have been written for physical as much as spiritual conflict. And whe
the Padre spoke, the soldiers turned their gaze up towards him. He was sayin
that this could be our last chance to reach an understanding with God.

In times of war men who would not step inside a church need to find an inne
strength and comfort. And that is what is happening among the Royal Scots. O
all the British Forces committed here, they are facing the greatest danger.
Trench warriors, they will be doing hand-to-hand fighting. Their targets will no
be seen from a cockpit or a tank turret, but face-to-face at the end of their SA80s
Now we are being told we could not choose when we died. "We need God for
peace and courage in the days ahead, but He is not an insurance policy," th
chaplain said. "It will require all of your inner strength, more than we have eve
had. People will die and have died on our side not because they lived a good o
bad life, but because mankind has got us into a war, because an evil has been
done. We have to put that evil right, and the price of it is the lives of soldiers. I
knowing what will happen, in knowing how many of us will die, we must ge
ourselves right with God. This may be our last opportunity, and we must do it a
we prepare for war, because He will look after our souls and give us help to
make us even better soldiers than we have trained to be. So we can go into ou
task in glory, honour and inner strength. For God inspires a deeper courage, «
deeper strength. "

When it was over, the queue for men wanting Communion too was as long
as that stretching from the Padre's truck awaiting sweets and cigarettes. It had
been a moment to savour, and afterwards we stood around in knots, all reluctan
to move. They say here that courage is like a bank balance. Today all of us
soldiers and non-combatants alike, received a boost to our reserves we wil
surely need in the days ahead.

Richard was wrong, in fact we were all wrong, in thinking that this might be
our last church service before we would be involved in combat. There would be
another three weeks before we would cross the breach and in that time we often
gathered together.

He was right, however, in submitting his dispatch and it resulted in a flurry
of reports. On Saturday, 2 February almost every national newspaper included
photos and text from that church service. Everything from the front page of the

aily Telegraph to page three of the Sun (Yes! Page 3 – not many men have managed that. A full-page spread all to myself.)

Mike Moore had submitted a number of photographs, many depicting our church service, with soldiers gathered round the Royal Stewart tartan communion table appeared in print, but the photo which obviously caught the editor's attention, and which went on to stir up much prayer around the country, was one of Cpl Brash.

Basil, as he was known to his mates (Basil = Basil Brush = Cpl Brash), was shown kneeling in the sand, dressed in desert combats with body armour and webbing, head bowed in prayer, a Church of Scotland soldier's prayer book held in his clasped hand and a rifle across his knees and helmet. For many folks back at home this image became the focus for their prayers. Here was one of their boys, connecting with his God, and they prayed for him as they prayed for all the troops.

A week or so later Basil committed his life to Christ. I was back at B Company selling goodies and taking Church again. I made a joke about people praying and getting on to the front of the newspaper. He came up to me afterwards and asked about the joke. It was obvious that something was troubling' him. He just felt a closeness to God that he couldn't shake off. "I think there are probably thousands of grannies back home praying for you because of those photographs. It sounds like the 'hound of heaven' is after you." And he prayed that day. Many would call it 'the believers' prayer'. He found a peace and a confidence that would help him in the days and years ahead.

That photograph still turns up from time to time. It hung on the wall in the Armed Forces chaplaincy Centre, Amport House and features in the Museum of army chaplaincy. It inspired my wife Christine to pen a poem. On the Saturday morning when all the newspapers included the report of our church service Christine had picked up her copy of *The Times* from the NAAFI in Werl, West Germany, before driving our four children to a toy shop to spend their pocket money. She was sitting in the car while the gang disappeared inside the shop. Imagine her surprise when she unfolded the paper to find her husband's picture.

The following poem was picked up by a number of organisations and publications, including the Church of Scotland's magazine *Life and Work*.

For Cpl Brash, 1RS
(and all who are heavy laden Matthew 11:28)

What thoughts pour through your head as you bow in silent prayer?
Do you know that there's a God of love behind the sorrow and despair?
With your rifle slung peacefully upon your bended knee,
I just wonder how much of the battle you actually can see.
As you kneel there on the sand, so many miles from home,
Despite your mates around you, you must really feel alone.
In the silence of the desert, as you kneel there in the sand,
Just ponder for a moment that Jesus is holding out his hand.
And in a place not far from there, he's also felt the same –
He too has knelt and prayed, in anguish and in pain.
He prayed he did not have to do what he'd been asked to do
But deep within his heart he knew that he'd have to see it through.
As the blood poured from his wounds as they hung him on the tree,
He knew quite well what loneliness was at that wretched Calvary.
And as he too looked to heaven, he knew a battled was being waged –
The war to beat all wars in the stillness round him raged.
And with the final torment of his soul, he quietly said, "Forgive."
The war was won that instant so that you and I might live.
Now Jesus stands beside you, with eyes that speak release.
He comes, a man of sorrow too, to give an everlasting peace.
There's not a burden in the world he won't know how to bear,
No suffering or sadness, or woe that he can't share.
There's not a sin so great that he hasn't paid the price –
He's reaching out to you now, the Saviour and the Christ.
And in the lull before the storm, he knows you'll do your best,
But still he says, "Come you who are heavy laden, and I will give you rest."

You can never do everything right, and as a clergyman your work is never completed. There are always other people to visit, you could always spend more time in prayer and study, a sermon could always be improved with more effort. It is no different on operations with the military. I often found this a real challenge on Operation BANNER in Northern Ireland. Finding the balance is difficult. You are always on duty, but not always in demand, always on call, at the end of a phone or radio, but not always with a clear list of tasks to fulfil. Your commander and his soldiers want to know that you can appear whenever they need to talk, but they certainly don't want to talk to you all the time.

Having said that, I found Op GRANBY less challenging in that way. Most nights I went to sleep tired after a long day's work but feeling that I had achieved all I could, and on the whole, I was satisfied that I served well throughout the operation. Yes, of course, I had frequent feelings that I could have preached better or counselled more effectively, but on the whole more satisfied with my ministry that I had been previously, and probably have been for a long time since.

The build-up to engaging with the enemy continued to intensify as we focussed on desert navigation rehearsals. There was a sense of expectation that each day was bringing us closer to the unavoidable. Any day now we would move north through the breach and come face to face with Saddam Hussein's military forces.

I spent quite a lot of time going round the various sub-units of the Battalion, making sure as far as possible, that I made myself available to talk to every soldier who wanted to chat. It was humbling to discover how many wanted to spend time with me, and how deeply they shared their fears and concerns. Conversations were usually one-to-one but not always. One day as I approached an eight-man team who were preparing their Warrior armoured vehicle for the battle, one of them asked, "Padre, will you say a prayer for us?"

"Of course, I will," I responded.

But when all eight of them knelt in the sand in a small tight circle, so that their padre could pray with them and for them, I could hardly get the words out. What a privilege.

My connection with the jocks was very precious, and often took me by surprise. Well, what took me most by surprise was their readiness to express their gratitude for what I was doing. I still have the letter signed by the RSM and the Provo Staff Team which moved me to tears of humility:

Padre

This is just a wee note to say thank you for everything you are doing for all the boys. You are so thoughtful and caring towards every single one of us and our families. You are a great support. You work so hard for us, and we all know that you don't have to do as much as you do.

Every time your Land Rover heads for one of our positions, wither it ↳
BG Main or A Coy or anyone else, all the lads are out saying, "Oh ye:
here's the Padre coming." You must be about the most popular man ↳
the Gulf.
So keep up the good work because we are all grateful, and once agair,
thank you.
That's from all of us S.F., J.S., J.B., S. M., A.L., and Oor Bob

The Ground War was getting closer and closer, and the CO's Orders Groups
giving clear military instructions for the next phase, became more intense, and
remember the atmosphere at the final one. This was it; this is what we had traine(
for, not just during the build-up to confront the Iraqi enemy, but what we had al
been preparing for since joining up. All the way through our military careers w(
had learnt our particular roles, used the Aides Memoire to create shape an(
structure, but it was no longer an exercise, this was for real, and you could cu
the atmosphere with a knife.

At last the commanding officer was finished, and it was time for questions
The need for complete understanding and total clarity meant that there were lot:
of questions, no one wanted to be even a little fuzzy about what was expected
The CO worked his way round the group and at last came to the doctor and ther
me. "Padre, any questions?"

"No questions, sir, but could you say all that again, I have no idea what you
were talking about!" Stupid comment? Perhaps, but everyone laughed, and i\
broke the tension. Joker in the pack? No one else could make a stupid comment,
we were about to go to war!

The next day, when I was dropping off some American MRE rations for the
CO's command vehicle, the commanding officer asked for a chat. Like all good
commanders he intended to address his men before he led us into battle, and he
had been working on his address. He wanted me to see the speech he had
prepared. I felt quite stunned by what I read, but it was clear that as our
commander he had a job to do, and part of that was to prepare us for the battle
ahead. There would be no more time to warm up, no extra time to get into gear.
As soon as the whistle blew, we must be ready to strike.

Richard Kay described the CO's message:

'His message was about killing. Short, sharp, to the point and very chilling. Unless the Iraqis had their hands up and wanted to surrender, they should be killed, he said. It was a policy to be pursued with absolute prejudice. If it couldn't be achieved with air strike, artillery or cannon fire, then use your rifle, he said. The bayonet was the last resort.'

I was a little taken aback, and I think the CO saw it in my reaction, so he xplained a bit further about his need to have men who were fully prepared and lert and ready to squeeze the trigger. Too long sitting about the desert waiting ould easily take the edge of their state of readiness.

As he explained this I wondered if perhaps I should be with him when he ddressed the troops, but he had clearly thought that all through. The next morning, we would hold a church service at each of the company locations. I ould conduct the service and then the men would 'about turn' and the Commanding officer would give his speech.

Let Richard Kay take up the story of the following morning...

Feb 23. In the darkness before the dawn the Siberian cold made you gasp. It was like opening the door of a butcher's freezer, and the wind was like a razor, slashing at your face. Over my tunic but beneath the body armour I put on an extra sweater, my last concession to civilian status. Padre Blakey, a committed Christian who despite his faith saw a right in waging war, had wrapped a black and white checked shemagh round his neck and was handing out prayer books. Before him a trestle table covered with a tartan rug and a travelling kit of sacraments. Deal cross and silver communion cup and standing beyond Royal Scots headquarters staff of 200 men, silhouetted in an orange glow from the fiery sun that was rising to replace the sight of the ugly angry flashes from the artillery. This was to be the last religious gathering. Together they said their Regimental Collect, but few shut their eyes, and this time the hymn singing was mute. When it was over, Iain Johnstone, who had been standing stiffly at the back, ordered the men to turn around. It seemed appropriate that after hearing God's word they should have their backs to the makeshift altar to listen to what their Colonel had to say.

We went round all the locations, following the same routine. There wasn much chat after the service and address. It suddenly felt very real. None of u knew what the next days would hold for us. Our future was in many ways beyon our control. All we could do was make sure that we were as prepared as possibl. So there was a lot of issuing of ammunition and rations and water, and in du course the wheeled vehicles all withdrew – including my driver Butch with th Land Rover. I think we were both quite sad to separate and made some stupi joke to cover our feelings.

As I was walking back toward the Regimental Air Post, a trooper from ou tank squadron approached me. "Is the Father around Padre?" (A question tha really only makes sense in the military world.)

"No, he's been here saying mass but has headed off back to the Fiel Hospital. You won't see him now until after the fighting. Can I help?"

"Well," he said, "my mother wrote and said that I wasn't to go into actio until the priest had blessed my tank. I suppose you would do." So, we headed o across the desert toward the squadron, their tanks camouflaged under dese scrim nets. On the way he produced from his pocket something that looked a first sight like an old Coca Cola bottle. "Oh, and she sent me this as well!" I turned out to be a bottle of Holy Water from Our Lady of Lourdes. *M grandmother will turn in her grave*, I thought, but just smiled and on we went.

I gathered the tank crew around, explained what I was going to do, sprinkle the Holy Water on the long barrel, and prayed the most evangelical prayer eve prayed over a piece of artillery… and the guys all said, "Amen!"

And it worked, you know. Oh, I don't know if it worked in the sense that i we hadn't blessed the tank it would have been destroyed by enemy fire. But i worked, as these important pastoral actions always work, in that it enabled tha soldier to go into action knowing that he had obeyed his mother, and his mothe was strengthened in her faith that God would protect her son.

I left the Cavalry guys to their thoughts and made my way back to th armoured ambulance that would be my home for the next few days. So, this wa it. Tonight, we were due to move north and form up along with the rest of th Brigade ready for the move into Iraq and whatever lay ahead.

It was a great honour to serve as chaplain to The Royal Scots and to serv alongside my fellow chaplains. Appendix E gives the ORBAT of 1RS on O GRANBY, and appendix F lists my fellow chaplains.

Chapter 7
Padre in Command

"For I myself am a man under authority, with soldiers under me. I tell this one, 'Go,' and he goes; and that one, 'Come,' and he comes. I say to my servant, 'Do this,' and he does it."

—*Gospel of Matthew 8:9*

Article 24 of the Geneva Convention of 1949 states that 'chaplains attached to the armed forces shall be respected and protected in all circumstances'. Chaplains are protected because their ministry to assist and support the religious and spiritual aspects of life is greatly valued. They themselves, and their activities, are regarded as 'supranational and quasi-neutral.' This protection applies at any place and at any time throughout the duration of an armed conflict on the battlefield and behind the lines.

These guidelines allow chaplains to be with their soldiers, near the front line and almost always co-located with the fighting unit's medical team. The medical team are armed so that they can protect themselves and their patients, but the chaplain remains unarmed.

Chaplains are, of course, only protected if they are formally attached to the armed forces in the role of chaplain. If a minister of a church were to join up or be recruited to normal army service, say in the infantry, and because of his training in Christian ministry was asked by his commanding officer to do some chaplaincy work from time to time, he would not be covered by the protection guaranteed by the Geneva Convention.

The requirement for the chaplain's role to be defined by the criteria of *attachment* and *exclusivity* results in the firm understanding that the Padre is always unarmed and never takes command.

Most of the time this understanding is unchallenged and does not cause confusion or friction. But there are times when the edges become a bit blurred. I have a distant memory, perhaps conveniently distant so I don't name and shame anyone in particular, of a whole batch of character-training pamphlets having to be destroyed because one of the photographs included the picture of an army chaplain on the streets of Belfast, patrolling with a four-man 'brick' and wearing a pistol in a holster. I imagine that his personal justification had something to do with his need to protect his own life, and his human right to do so. This argument raises its head from time to time, and most recently by a Royal Marine chaplain in Afghanistan, serving with the army, and who was not at all happy when instructed to get rid of the pistol, being told that 'it's not what we do'.

When Jim Harkness was chaplain general, he oversaw a change in the RAChD Dress Regulations, which define the various uniforms worn by chaplains. Previously in our more formal Service Dress Uniform we wore a Sam Browne belt in common with many other units. This leather belt was designed to enable the wearer to carry a sword hanging from the waist. Highly polished it is quite an elegant addition to the uniform.

Chaplains are unarmed and therefore don't carry a sword in any order of uniform. It was felt that a cross belt with a pouch on the back would be more

ppropriate than a belt designed for carrying a sword. The pouch is symbolic of
arrying a message which is an important aspect of chaplaincy. The dress
egulations were duly changed. I have to say, however, that the Sam Browne belt
lways seemed more elegant to me, but perhaps this is because as my waistline
ncreased the Sam Browne helped to hold me together whereas the cross belt
eemed to highlight the growing paunch.

It is not always easy to keep everyone happy, but chaplains need to try and
lo so, and when we fail there is very often a record of the occurrence somewhere
n a filing cabinet.

In September 2017, the chaplain general kindly came to my civilian church
n Duns in Berwickshire to preach at the Sunday service which marked the 40th
nniversary of my ordination and commissioning. He opened his sermon by
quoting from the reference which Dr John Thomson, rector of Madras College,
St Andrews had written in support of my application to join RAChD. I was very
mpressed that this piece of paper was still in my Personnel File and pleased that
Dr John had said such nice things about me, but I did feel a shiver make its way
lown my back when I thought of some of the other material which that file must
contain. As I look back over these past 40 years, I realise that there is a list, quite
a long list, which could be headed 'Things I really should not have done' and
which would include one or two occasions when I found myself taking command
of a situation.

Some of the entries in my own list of 'things I really should not have done'
would include times when my sense of humour wasn't as well received as I had
hoped, such as the incident which occurred during our pre-deployment build up
for a forthcoming Operation BANNER Tour in South Armagh, Northern Ireland.
We were training at the NITAT (Northern Ireland Training and Advisory Team)
Centre at Lydd and Hythe on the south coast of England. Our tour was going to
be in the very dangerous area on the Irish border, known to the soldiers as Bandit
Country. I would be based at Bessbrook, in the old mill, and during my six
months all of my travel to visit our company locations (such a Crossmaglen,
Forkhill and the various towers and observation posts) would be by helicopter.
The troops however would be on the ground patrolling on foot the territory that
was often controlled by the Provisional IRA. The Company Commander of
XMG (Crossmaglen) was keen on taking an aggressive stance, ensuring that the
terrorists knew full well who was in control, and had ordered his soldiers to cover
their weapons with camouflage patterned masking tape. It certainly did add to a

warlike image and turned the normal black metal and plastic rifle surfaces int DPM (distorted pattern material) like our combat uniforms.

A bit of a conflict had arisen between the battalion officers about whether o not all the other rifle companies should follow suit, and if so, who should pay fo the many rolls of patterned masking tape. There was grumbling in the officers mess on the Saturday evening prior to our early morning Sunday Church Muste The next morning, I came on to parade with my clerical collar camouflaged wit the very same tape, much to the annoyance of a certain major, and the amusemen of everyone else. In retrospect it was not the wisest move. Said major was no my biggest fan, and I had just made things worse!

Humour plays an important part in military life. In the darkest of moments and in the fog of war, humour can lift the spirits and save the mind fron becoming overwhelmed by the horror of events. For chaplains, and I guess al leaders, humour can also be a really powerful tool for connecting intellectuall and emotionally with the soldiers. It is a well-recognised skill in public speakin; reflected in the saying, 'The audience that laughs with you also listens to you.'

Humour does need to be exercised carefully paying regard to the compan and the setting. Early on in the second half of my military career, starting off a. a chaplain in the Territorial Army, I needed to find a block of seven days trainin; so that I could qualify for my annual bounty. (Bounty is a tax-free payment mad(to Reserve Forces personnel who complete the government agreed level o training each year.) Rev Iain Barclay, serving as Staff Chaplain Headquarters 2ⁿ Division, based in Craigiehall on the north side of Edinburgh, and a good frien(since our days together at university, came to my rescue and organised a five-day course at the Armed Forces Chaplaincy Centre, Amport House, followed by a preaching engagement at Sunday morning worship at St Andrew's Garrison Church, Aldershot. The resident chaplain was fellow Church of Scotlanc chaplain Rev John Dailly.

John was a good friend. I was looking forward to preaching in his church, and he was pleased not to have to prepare a sermon for that Sunday. The congregation that day was quite large. In addition to his normal congregation of 60 or so folk, there was the usual smattering of senior officers and a good-sized squad of soldiers who had been marched there as part of the training course the were attending.

My sermon was about God as a Covenant-making God, and the Old Testament lesson from Genesis chapter 15 included the list of Canaanite tribes, he Kenites, Kenizzites, Kadmonites, Hittites, Perizzites, Rephaites, Amorites, 'anaanites, Girgashites and Jebusites.'

I drew the congregation's attention to these wonderful names. "Aren't these xcellent tribal names?" as I read them out again, rolling my r's. Sensing some esponse from the soldiers in the pews, I went on, "Imagine walking down auchiehall Street in Glasgow on a Saturday night and meeting one of these guys. See you, you wee Girgashite!' has a certain feel to it, does it not?"

I glanced over and saw John sliding down in his chair and sensed that he vasn't as amused as some of the younger members of the congregation seemed ɔ be. His concern was I suspect more about the senior general sitting on the front ew. The general made no comment over the cup of tea in the church hall fterwards, but John did suggest that he would be vetting my sermon the next ime I preached for him. There was no next time.

In those days, Aldershot was the largest British army Garrison in the world nd St Andrew's Garrison Church was regarded a bit as the Church of Scotland nilitary cathedral. There has been a Church of Scotland in Aldershot since the nid-nineteenth century. By a strange coincidence one of my predecessors in my resent parish in Angus had served in Aldershot in what was then known as 'the ron Church'. Rev Francis Nicoll Cannan was the minister of Lintrathen Parish Church when in May 1855 he responded to a public call for chaplains to support he troops in the Crimea in the then role of assistant chaplain. On his return from Crimea he made the decision to apply for a full commission and served on in the rmy chaplains Department until he retired in 1875 aged 64 with the rank haplain to the Forces Class 1, the equivalent of colonel.

The only other army chaplain to also have been minister of what is now The sla Parishes (The Church of Scotland Parish Church which covers the previous arishes of Airlie, Glenisla, Kilry, Kingoldrum, Lintrathen and Ruthven) was Rev Ivan Warwick. Ivan and I had studied theology together at New College, Edinburgh, and he was tight head prop for the New College Lions rugby team vhen I was the captain and hooker. We were a pretty powerful team with an aggressive approach to destroying the opposition in the intra-mural league of Edinburgh University. Other teams did not like to be drawn against us because he games were usually rather bruising events, and we almost always won except when playing against the Christian Union team. The annual fixture was known as the Christians against the Lions, and annoyingly the Christian Union Christians almost always won. We always put it down to their supporters praying fervently on the touch line. Spiritual warfare wasn't a high priority for theolog students, though perhaps it should have been.

After his first parish appointment in Lintrathen Ivan joined as a regular arm chaplain. Although he only served a few years as a regular he then becam involved with the army cadet Force and still serves both as an ACF chaplain an an officiating chaplain to the military, providing support to the regular arm chaplain based at Fort George, near Inverness.

Many people in the parish remember Ivan warmly, though I have been tol a less than flattering story about his horse and the local pub which reminded m a bit of Tam's ride home from the pub in Robert Burns' poem *Tam O'Shanter*. questioned Ivan recently about this. We were having lunch in the officers' mes of Edinburgh Castle during the general assembly of the Church of Scotland. "Di you have a horse when you were minister of Lintrathen?" I asked.

"That's a strange question," he replied, "why do you ask?"

"Well I was visiting one of your old parishioners recently, and she recounte a story about some minister only getting home from the pub safely because h horse knew the way! She couldn't remember the minister's name. I wondered i it might be you."

"Naw, wasn't me. I did have a horse, but it was the wrong horse." Not reall understanding his reply I decided to just let the matter go. Friendship is mor important than getting the full story 'from the horse's mouth'.

Like Ivan Warwick, and many of my other colleagues, I was very aware tha a good bit of a chaplain's time is spent just 'being there' while the rest of th army goes about its business. This is part of our incarnational ministry, and ofte leads to really good conversations with soldiers who in a relaxed setting can fee freer to talk openly about the deeper things of life. It can also, of course sometimes leave the chaplain feeling that no useful contribution is being made Chaplains are intelligent, well-educated men and women, with their ow leadership skills and abilities, and it can be difficult to keep all of that containe within a role that is undefined and at times undemanding.

This is not a new problem for chaplains. During the First World War, on chaplain found himself becoming an expert in operating a field X-Ray machine He was located in a medical unit which had an X-ray and a specialist doctor i charge of it. One day the doctor's assistant took ill, and as the only person whc seemed to have nothing else to do, the padre was roped in to assist for the day During the afternoon some emergency arose, and the specialist doctor wa ordered back to the field hospital. He handed over to another doctor with the words, "The padre knows what to do!" And so the padre became the expert, and was frequently called upon to assist in a role which was certainly not part of his training nor his calling.

Many chaplains have discovered that having some areas of responsibility beyond the spiritual and ecclesiastical spheres helps to fulfil their role, and sometimes to fill the day. If the chaplain can share some responsibility, support the unit, help facilitate the commanding officer's plans without denying his own role, then that can be a win-win situation for all concerned.

There is of course the danger of a new chaplain arriving in unit and having to live up to, or compete with, the reputation of his predecessor. "Padre so-and-so used to take part in the weekly combat run, and usually came in first." Padre so-and-so might well become a 'right so-and-so' in his successors mind. I always reckoned it was much better to take over from a fellow chaplain who had been a bit of a disaster. (Not that any of my predecessors ever were – in case you are wondering who I am talking about!)

When Rev Angus Kerr moved from regular to reserve chaplaincy, he found himself replacing a colleague who had built a reputation of personally publishing a very impressive daily newspaper while on the annual two-week summer camp with this particular TA unit. Angus quickly discovered that he was expected to continue with what had now become a tradition, and that if he didn't then he would struggle to get access to transport to visit the troops out on the training area. He had to explain in great detail that the transport was provided so that he could do his job as a chaplain, and not so that he could gather stories for the newspaper. It took time, but he won and got his Land Rover.

Chaplaincy does not really lend itself to leadership and my main on-going opportunity to exercise any innate leadership ability during my 16 years regular army service was on the rugby park. Throughout my regular military service, I was more often than not the rugby officer for the unit to which I was attached. Apart from that I seldom exercised anything that could be described as leadership. That was until a unique opportunity came my way in Berlin in 1988.

It was a Wednesday afternoon, the time of the week that is traditionally a sports afternoon in army units. The gladiators would take to whichever field they were skilled at and work off some of their aggression against a team from another unit. For some reason I wasn't involved in sport that day, and so I had planned to head off home early.

I was on my way off out of camp when I decided to wander through battalio headquarters to see if anyone was working in the offices and found the adjutan sitting at his desk looking somewhat stressed. It was coming up to what wa sometimes called the 'silly season' in Berlin with all sorts of unit, national an international parades and events. Personnel had to be found to man all thes parades and duties. A list of requirements was passed down from brigad headquarters and each unit was tasked to fill all the slots allocated to it. Thi responsibility fell on the shoulders of the adjutant, and the burden of thi responsibility was clearly weighing heavily on Mike, who I am sure would hav much preferred to be outside enjoying sports afternoon to sitting at his des trying to balance staffing lists and spreadsheets.

"I need to find a commander for the British Military Train on Friday. Nobod is available, and I need a captain or major," he mumbled, before looking up witl a glint in his eye and declaring, "you could do it, Padre!" Well, perhaps I coul do all that was required, but I definitely SHOULD NOT! We bantered back and forth a bit, before I gave in. What was the worst that could happen? Apart from an international incident and the very rapid end to both of our military careers?

The British Military Train (BMT) travelled daily from West Berlin, through East Germany to West Germany, and then returned in the evening. This was in 1988 prior to the end of the cold war and the collapse of the Berlin wall in 1989 The city of Berlin sat like an island in the middle of Communist East Germany (The German Democratic Republic) 145 miles from the border with West Germany (The Federal Republic of Germany). At the end of the second World War the city was divided into four sectors which were allocated to USSR, USA France and the UK. West Berlin comprised the American, French and Britist sectors, and was divided at this time from East Berlin by the Berlin Wall.

Nikita Krushchev, one-time leader of the Soviet Union, is quoted as saying that the city of Berlin was 'the testicles of the West. When I want the West to scream, I squeeze Berlin.' The divided city represented the state of play at the end of the Second World War, frozen in time. Some would say that War only finally ended when the Wall came down in November 1989

Before then each of the allied nations had internationally agreed road and rail corridors from West Berlin to West Germany. These were carefully controlled and monitored and keeping them open was an important political statement which reminded the Warsaw Pact powers that we had this right of access through East Germany. On top of the political posturing the train provided a very pleasant ay out of the city for British military personnel and families based in Berlin. An armed military guard travelled in the daily train and I was going to be the commander.

Chaplains had a unique dress policy protocol in Berlin which allowed us to wear a normal officer's khaki shirt and tie, rather than the clerical collar stated in the RAChD Service Dress Regulations, when visiting East Berlin. This allowed us to blend in better and avoided us drawing attention to our religious status. I don't know how official this policy was, but it did mean that as commander of the BMT I looked more like a regular officer than a padre.

Serving in Berlin as occupying powers, and the associated access to Communist East Berlin, provided a very privileged opportunity to see 'behind the iron curtain'. It was clear that the Soviet Block engaged in a certain level of window dressing in East Berlin, and so the picture was distorted to some degree, but even with that distortion the stark contrast between Capitalist West Berlin and Communist East Berlin was clear to see. Someone once said that if you could stand on the Berlin Wall and look west you would see a picture painted in beautiful technicolour but if you looked east it was a picture of just shades of grey.

One of the most fascinating seasons to be in East Berlin was Christmas. While the whole Biblical story was regarded as a fairy tale in Communist propaganda, they still celebrated the season of Christmas. It was the one time of the year when the large plate glass windows in the shops near Alexander Platz were richly decorated, often showcasing the most beautiful Victorian era nativity scenes. They were a wonder to behold, but perhaps what was more remarkable was the confidence of the political regime which allowed the displays in shop windows, seeing it as no threat to their anti-religion doctrine. During the rest of the year most of these shop windows were drab and pretty empty.

My day in command of the train ran smoothly. Christine and I had a lovely day out. I managed to dig up some of my school-boy Russian and had a brief conversation with the Russian officer who inspected our passports, and we returned safely to the British sector of Berlin with no incidents and no damage to our careers. Mike Riddell-Webster was until recently the Governor of Edinburgh Castle and I suspect has forgotten all about this.

My other surprising opportunity to command troops came a couple of years later while serving with the Royal Scots in the first Gulf War. During the 100 hours of the ground battle I was located in the Regimental Aid Post along with our two medical officers and the other members of the team. We travelled in two armoured ambulances which were converted tracked APCs (Armoured Personnel Carriers). They looked sort of like tanks with no gun on top.

During the second night of the fighting we were speeding through an enemy position, travelling fast to keep pace with the rest of the battalion, when our vehicle thumped into an enemy tank trench. We were driving with no lights so as to avoid being seen by the Iraqis and our driver saw the large hole in the ground too late to avoid it, and in we went. The vehicle was sitting at an awkward angle, but even more worrying was the fact that we had thrown both its caterpillar tracks.

The decision was quickly made, and the doctor and medical sergeant were picked up by the other armoured ambulance which then disappeared off rapidly into the dark to catch up with the battalion headquarters' vehicles, leaving me and the rest of the crew behind.

We sat there in the silence for a few moments as it slowly dawned on us that we were very much on our own. The whole Royal Scot battlegroup had disappeared over the horizon leaving us with our 432 tracked ambulance sitting at a jaunty angle in the middle of an Iraqi position. The group consisted of myself, a corporal (the driver), a lance-corporal (the radio operator) and a private soldier. 'Now what?' was the question in our minds as we peered out of the back door of the vehicle at the disturbing shadows and silhouettes that were appearing as our eyesight grew used to the darkness and the first glow of the sunrise started to change the tone of the night sky.

One of my team cocked his rifle and said, "Let's go and see what's out there! We cannae just sit here like sitting ducks!" He was all for heading off to explore what were clearly enemy vehicles of various shapes and sizes all within a 100 yards radius.

"We're not going anywhere, and certainly not until the sun comes up," I declared with more confidence than I felt. "We've no idea what's out there, so we're staying put, close to our vehicle." Three soldiers, three rifles, even as a padre I knew a wee bit about arcs of fire and defensive positions. I was of course unarmed, so I was totally dependent on them doing what I asked of them. I took command of the situation and allocated responsibilities and arcs to each man and told them to stay alert and wait to see what would happen.

Nothing happened. The sun came up, bringing some welcome warmth to our chilled bodies and improving our view of where we actually were. The vehicle ad in fact thrown its track as it crossed a sort of trench designed to lower the rofile of an Iraqi vehicle so that it could still function while not being easily isible. All around us were similar trenches, some empty but many occupied by variety of command vehicles and pieces of artillery. It had clearly been bandoned. There was no sign of life, though I didn't allow the guys to explore oo carefully or too widely. My priority was to get our vehicle roadworthy as oon as possible so that we could catch up with the rest of the battlegroup before ne next night's fighting. I was well aware that the crew of broken-down vehicles vere usually picked up by our own side and back loaded away from the attlefield. There was no room for extra bodies, so if you lost your own vehicle ou had to withdraw from the front line. I was determined that this wasn't going o happen to me, and some fairly strong language persuaded my fellow crew nembers that no matter how much effort it might take we would get these tracks ack on the vehicle and we would catch up with the other ambulance before last ight.

And we did. We were visited by a number of friendly forces during the norning. Some were for giving us a lift back to Royal Scots, an echelon where Butch was located with my Land Rover and our other wheeled vehicles. They vere firmly told what to do with that idea. One visitor provided a hot meal, and vhen we were back in a roadworthy condition, another led us back 'home' to Battalion headquarters. It would be too strong to say that we were welcomed varmly, more of a 'What took you so long?' But we were back, and ready for hat final night which would see victory.

It was good to have a guide to help us meet up with the rest of the Battalion. Finding your way round the desert was not easy. We were operating far away rom any roads and the occasional wadi was just about all that was marked on he maps. Satellite Navigation was a fairly new concept in these days, and only those and such as those' had access to one, so we had to learn desert navigation. When I say, "We had to learn," I mean that I heard it talked about from time to ime.

I managed to find my way around fairly well and never got really lost, and on one occasion found myself showing others the way.

It was on 24 January 1991. There was a major unit move about to happen. The men of 1 Royal Scots were going to be flown by Hercules transport plane and Chinook helicopters to our new location. The armoured vehicles would be moved by transporter, and Butch and I were to travel in our Land Rover as part of the road convoy. I attended the 'O' Group and knew that at a certain time was to join the wheeled vehicle convoy at a designated Release Point.

The instructions all sounded fairly straightforward. All we had to do was follow the vehicle in front, whose driver was probably doing exactly the sam (playing 'Follow my leader') and trusting that whoever was in the lead positic would get us to the correct destination. I had no idea where that might be b learnt later that it was an important element in confusing the enemy by launchi our eventual attack from a location much further west that he was expecting.

As we still had a few hours to spare Butch and I decided to take tl opportunity to restock our mobile shop. Supplies were running low and we ha no idea when we might next have the opportunity to visit a shop or garage. W had noticed a garage slightly north of our position – up toward Basra – so mi afternoon we headed off with our wad of cash to see what we could buy. Tl garage shop was very well stocked, and we filled up the back of the wagon wil all sorts of goodies before heading back to the Battle Group to find our rig place in the long line of vehicles which was gathering in the dusk.

We were tight for time; it was all a bit rushed and a little tense. I don't kno if we had added to the tension by actually being a bit late, but Butch just followe the somewhat blunt instructions and got his 'f***ing wagon' into line. And : usual, it was a case of "Hurry up and wait!"

It got darker and colder as dusk turned to night, and slowly we move forward little by little. I was feeling pretty disorientated, but I knew that all Butc and I had to do was to just follow the vehicle in front, and all would be well. took about four hours, from eight o'clock in the evening until about midnight t reach the convoy release point.

We were slowly shunting forward when suddenly, out of the darkness, Royal Military Police corporal appeared holding up a hand-held stop sign, lik the ones used by German police. "Stop and report to the tent over there," h called out to me.

"No, I need to keep following that vehicle," I replied in some desperation.

"No, this is the start of a new packet and you are the lead vehicle."

"No, no, no, I am the padre, I don't lead, can't you just let me through…" pleaded as the convoy lights of the wagon up ahead disappeared into the gloon

"Sir, just go over to the tent and talk to the major."

And so, I did as commanded (the earlier request seemed to have changed into a command, and we all know never to disobey an RMP command) – "they will get their man!"

"Look, something's gone wrong here with this package. I don't know where 'm going. I haven't got a map."

The major in the tent was really helpful. "Padre, you don't need a map. You've got three minutes before you start. There isn't time to do anything else. Just follow the route, drive at 20 km an hour, and at each change of direction one of my men will be there to point the way."

So I got back into the Land Rover, and said to Butch, "We're leading this package but don't worry, there's no problem; just drive at 20 kph and we'll be fine."

"The speedo's bust, Boss!" he replied.

So off we headed, feeling more than a little nervous – not so much for myself – but for the dozen vehicles innocently following on behind, trusting that I knew where I was going and probably really pleased that if we got totally lost it would not be their responsibility.

We drove throughout the night and most of the next morning. It was, in fact, just a case of following the route and most of the route was a long straight road leading from East to West taking us further and further from the sea, from where I believe we had persuaded Saddam Hussein the main allied attack would come. But even a long straight road can become a bit worrying when there is just pitch blackness ahead of you, hour after hour. Driving along in a stripped-down Land Rover wrapped up in as much clothing as we could get on, with our ponchos carefully arranged so that the hot air from the Land Rover heater blew up inside and warmed our bodies, was an interesting experience, never to be repeated.

The Breakfast Stop in the morning gloaming was a wonderful relief for all sorts of reasons. We caught up with the earlier packets of Royal Scots vehicles, ate a hot breakfast prepared by the army chefs, and rested briefly before moving on. Each vehicle had two drivers so no real need for a long break. I was fully expecting that our Officer Commanding A2 Echelon, Capt Bill McGrath, would be impressed that I had managed to lead my packet to the right location and would willingly replace my slot up front with someone more qualified for the rest of the journey. No chance. I was told to stop being such a wimp and to get back behind the wheel and hurry up, I was holding people back.

In the daylight we began to see signs of life – mainly military life but also some Saudi population – and within a couple of hours we were led off the tarmac road onto sandy gravel routes, Main Supply Routes (MSR's) which had been laid out by the Americans, I think. By early afternoon we were in our new location, with a renewed sense of expectation that the attack into Iraq was now only a few days off.

One evening at 'stand to' there was a knock on the door of the armoured ambulance I shared with Dr John Timothy. It was a fellow padre, Philip Majcher who wasn't quite sure where he was. He had travelled rather further north from his own unit the Royal Scots Dragoon Guards than he had intended and now wasn't quite sure how to get home. In truth if he had continued in his present direction, he would have eventually been stopped by the huge sand berms which Saddam Hussein has created to stop us crossing over into Kuwait and Iraq. So once 'stand to' was over we pointed him South towards the Main Supply Route (MSR) which would take him home. "Just keep the moon over your left shoulder and you will be fine," we assured him. He looked doubtful, and years later when I tried to tease him for being lost in the desert and heading at speed towards the enemy, he suggested it was all in my imagination!

A couple of days later my own reputation for navigating in the desert took a sudden, but probably very short-lived, improvement. Butch and I had taken a considerable number of orders for Desert Teddies and Interflora Flowers, and we really needed to get back to Al Jubal where there was a field post office, so that we could process the orders. A couple of the Regimental clerks had come north from B Echelon to do some administration with the jocks. Butch and I decided to hitch a ride back with them in the comfort of their Toyota land cruiser rather than bumping along in our stripped-down Land Rover.

When they started off following the long and winding MSR, which went through a multitude of unit locations and was in some places full of ruts and often slowed down with a traffic jam, we offered to take over the driving and to show them a quicker route. Our route was over virgin desert with nothing in sight, but endless gravel covered flat sand, with the occasional tumbleweed rolling across our path. It was magnificent – open desert, untouched by human hand, undisturbed by warlike preparations going on to our North. The two clerks, strapped in the back seat of their 'hijacked' vehicle, looked very much as if we were getting them lost in the land of no return.

"Padre, do you know where we are? Shouldn't we go back and follow the Main Supply Route, as ordered by Capt Sutherland?"

"No, no, it's okay, no need to worry. I know exactly where we are and if we keep the sun at just that angle, we will hit the tarmac road spot on." And Butch pushed the accelerator harder to the deck.

Half an hour later we did hit that road. Spot on. Now the road was about 200 miles long, East to West, and we were travelling South. There was no way we could miss the road, but we kept that quiet and let them be impressed with the Padre's desert navigation for a wee while at least.

Command is not part of our calling as chaplains though we do, of course, have our own chain of command in RAChD all the way up to the chaplain general. I have never been in a situation where I was eligible for promotion above CF3 (Chaplain to the Forces class 3 = Major). I left the regular army aged 40, two years too young for promotion, though I did have a few weeks as 'Senior Chaplain Foot and Mouth' but more of that later.

Chapter 8
The Family Came Too

"How lucky I am to have something that makes saying goodbye so hard." — *A.A Milne*

I joined an army which was well used to soldiers and officers being married and expecting their families to accompany them. Most of the married personnel were 'married accompanied' which meant that we took our spouses and children with us to whichever location we were posted whether in the UK or overseas and the family lived together in a married quarter provided by the military usually located near the barracks and for which a very reasonable rent was paid by the occupants. 'Married unaccompanied' individuals had, on the whole, left their families in their own houses while they themselves lived in the service accommodation provided for the single personnel.

The arrangement was regarded by most of us as pretty satisfactory. It had adapted over many decades and worked well. The fact that it was very dependent on a cohort of military wives who were willing to be treated in a somewhat offhand and military fashion seldom raised its head as an issue, and we all just got on with it.

There were a few downsides. Married quarters came as either furnished or unfurnished, and like many other couples, Christine and I started off with a fully furnished quarter in the late 70s. All the basics were provided. Tables, chairs, beds, crockery and cutlery, cooker, bedding and towels, carpets and curtains This was wonderful for newly married couples who probably had very little in the way of their own furniture. When you took over your new home you were 'marched in'. Everything was counted and inspected. Assuming all was well you signed for your quarter, and it became your new home. You were given a couple of days to raise any complaints or concerns.

Quarters were usually immaculate and very few complaints were made at 'march in'. Having said that we did have to ask the Housing Warden to call out Rentokil to deal with the mice we discovered in our daughter's bedroom in our first army house.

The wonderful clean condition of houses at 'march in' was easily explained by the astonishing amount of work to be done in preparing a quarter for the 'march out' which was required when the time came for you to hand the house back to the housing warden and his team. Seasoned army wives became experts at all sorts of dark arts such as soaking the inner surface plates of the cooker in the bath for a couple of days to remove all signs of normal everyday usage and using toothpaste or baking dough to fill in the holes made by hanging too many pictures on the walls. We were once fined for leaving too many holes along one wall. I don't think the maximum number allowed actually appeared anywhere in print but was left to the humour and goodwill of the team conducting the 'march out'.

'Marching out' of an army married quarter could be a very unsettling experience. The property and its contents were inspected before you were free to leave, and getting away from the house was vital because your departure almost always involved a move to a new location or even a new country. Having moved out of the quarter the family was temporarily homeless and probably feeling pretty tired and vulnerable. It didn't help to calm the nerves if, for example, you were unfortunate enough to have a Housing Warden who appeared with a torch to inspect the inside of the cooker, or white gloves to check the tops of the wardrobes.

Our worst 'march out' was in Osnabruck when we were being allowed to move from a captain's quarter with three bedrooms to a major's quarter with four, which was a more suitable house for our family with three children. The move became more complex than it needed to be when a major from the battalion I was serving with decided that he preferred the house on a side street which we were being offered, to his existing one which was on a main road. He decided that he would move into the vacant house, and we could then have the main road one. On top of this the British Forces Education Service (BFES) teacher who had been allocated the captain's quarter, which we were moving out of, complained that he was being discriminated against, and tried to demand that he got the now-vacant major's quarter on the main road instead of us.

It seemed to have all cooled down, and our 'march out' and the teacher 'march in' were both planned to happen simultaneously on 1 August, during the KOSB Minden Day Parade. I had to be on parade, and so Christine was left with the three children to 'march out'. We were planning to attend the Minden Day lunch in the officers' mess and then head straight off to Norway for two weeks leave with Christine's parents.

I came off parade to find a very upset wife and a furious families' officer. The teacher had turned down our quarter on the basis that the cellar floor had not been properly swept and that he had found a ten Pfennig coin in a drawer of the sideboard. The families' officer promised to 'sweep the bloody cellar' himself over the weekend and so as to ensure that the teacher accepted the house on Monday morning, "You go off and enjoy your leave, Padre!"

In between the 'march in' and the 'march out', families had the joy of living in a house which had the same carpet pattern, same curtain material, same wall colouring and same crockery design as all of the neighbours. Necessity being the mother of invention did turn generations of military wives into budding interior designers with great skills ranging from making loose covers to personalise the sofa, to producing new curtains to replace the ones supplied by the military, and of course therefore the ability to resize them from the previous quarter to fit every new house on each posting.

Soon after moving onto the officers' patch in Redford were invited next door for supper one evening. Another newly married officer and his wife were also invited. You can imagine the dismay of this new wife when she discovered that the pattern they had chosen as their good dinner set as a wedding gift was the same pattern, though perhaps a different quality, to the crockery provided in every quarter on the patch.

The provision of housing for military families has changed in many ways over the decades. I think on the whole Christine and I were just grateful for a nice home and probably too busy with work and children to worry about the inconveniences and annoyances. (Or that might just be a male perspective!) Our first two quarters were in Edinburgh and Inverness, and the removal from one to the other was pretty much as it would have been for a civilian, except that the military picked up the tab. Our next move was to open up a whole new view of military life.

Christine had just given birth to our third child, and so really had enough to do looking after Barbara (3½), Malcolm (2) and Caroline (2 months) without worrying about the challenges of a military move from Inverness to Osnabruck. There was plenty to think about. We had, for instance, to buy a new tax-free car. The 'had to' was down to the state of my existing ten-year-old Vauxhall Viva combined with the peer pressure from the hundreds of others in the unit driving around in their shiny new motors and the car salesmen who seemed to hang around like vultures waiting for the next individual's resistance to weaken before swooping in for the kill – well 'sale'.

As a married Captain I had a set allocation for MFO (Movement of Forces Overseas) boxes which would allow us to move a fair amount of household and personal belongings to Germany, and then everything else, well everything else up to my storage allocation, would be put into store, which would also be paid for by the MOD. It was a well thought-out and well-practised process, but it was jolly hard work and emotionally draining. Even constructing the boxes was a challenge. They came flat packed but without the technology of Ikea. The tops and bottoms had to be screwed in place resulting in blistered palms from overworked screwdrivers.

Once all the boxes had been constructed, filled, contents recorded on a manifest, and the top screwed down, a team of soldiers arrived with a four-ton truck and collected them for delivery to Fort George, where they would be loaded onto a shipping container for the move overseas. We watched with a degree of horror as our precious possessions were loaded on to the truck with all the care of airport baggage staff, and wondering what state it would all arrive in.

While the MFO allocation was pretty generous the officers' mess had arranged for an extra container for any officer who had gone over their allocation. We had done pretty well dividing up everything between what was going with us and what was staying in store but we weren't at all sure what to do with the lovely Bechstein upright piano that Christine had inherited from her grandfather. There was space on this extra container and, in what was perhaps a moment of madness, we decided to go for it and to take the piano with us. The sight of it being wheeled down the road to be loaded into the container did make us wonder if we had made the correct decision.

Christine enjoyed having her piano with her in Germany but it became a challenge again with our next move, which was to Hong Kong. For this posting we had an even smaller MFO allocation and as it was an individual posting there was no over-allocation container. The piano ended up in store after all, along with other additional belongings which we had to send back to store in the UK before we headed off to the Far East.

* * * * *

Our first night in Osnabruck was spent lodging with the senior chaplain, Rev Tom Hiney MC. Tom and his wife Muriel very kindly accommodated the five of us when we arrived, tired and bedraggled, after a few days' holiday in Luxemburg en route to Germany. I'm not sure how much good the holiday did us, but it had seemed a good idea at the time. Caroline was born about eight weeks before we left Inverness, and Christine and baby could probably have done without all the travel and the temporary holiday accommodation. My main memory of the holiday was of trying to avoid letting our three-year-old Barbara realise that the hundreds of sweet little bunnies hopping about in a hillside enclosure were not someone's favourite pets but were in fact destined for the cooking pot. "Why has he got so many pets, Daddy?"

Osnabruck was, in those days, the largest British army garrison outside the UK. The Kings Own Scottish Borderers was just one of five major units which, alongside two brigade headquarters and all the assorted minor units, created a huge British community. Although I had been in the chaplains' department for over three years by this time, this was the family's first proper contact with the army medical services, the army library service, the NAAFI, Church Army, British Forces Post Office, the BFG (British Forces Germany) vehicle registration and testing system, British Forces Education Service and many more entities which would support, shape and at times control, our family life for a number of years.

The military system worked extraordinarily well, but it did have its idiosyncrasies. We did almost all of our shopping at the Navy, Army and Air Force Institutes (NAAFI). This organisation had been created by the government in 1920 and had a dual function of running both recreational clubs and shopping facilities for British service personal and their families. In its heyday the NAAFI ran clubs in every British barracks round the world, as well as shops and supermarkets in every garrison. The inside of the NAAFI shop in Germany looked just like the inside of the NAAFI in UK. It felt like home territory and sold goods which we all recognised. This familiarity meant that most Brits shopped at the NAAFI rather than in local German shops.

One of the idiosyncrasies was that the purchase of tea and coffee from the NAAFI required the use of a ration card, which also covered cigarettes, gin and whisky. This was a way of avoiding anyone taking advantage of our duty-free status. Petrol likewise was tax free, so we had to buy coupons in camp, which we then presented as payment at certain designated German petrol stations.

All of this, of course, impacted on our wives and families. Christine returned from her first visit to the Garrison Library somewhat annoyed that she wasn't allowed to join in her own right. She was a 'wife of' and needed my army number in order to be enrolled. No one had asked her for it back in UK, but she learnt the six-digit number that day and can still quote it.

Every part of our lives seemed to be under the protecting but sometimes stifling umbrella of the army. The doctor was an army doctor, you collected your daily newspaper from the Church Army, you lived on a 'patch' of army quarters where all your neighbours were also in the army, you shopped in the NAAFI, you heard the news on British Forces Broadcasting Service radio and the military choose which programmes would be shown on BFBS television, having rented your television from SSVC shop (Services Sound and Vision Corporation). There was a lot of camaraderie and the social life was excellent, but it was sometimes difficult to just be yourselves.

Wives (because 'spouses' were mainly 'wives' in the 1970s and 80s) were an important part of military life in general, and regimental life in particular. The story of an officer, separated from his wife at the time his name appeared on the pink list (the list of majors selected for promotion to Lt colonel), who was told that the only way he would be considered for command of his regiment would be if his wife accompanied him for the duration of the tour in Germany, was quite possibly true. You didn't need to have a wife to command, but it was a great benefit if you did, and if you didn't then other officers' wives would have to stand in on a frequent basis, for such tasks as heading up the wives' club, arranging flower displays for royal visits to the officers' mess, and hosting dinner parties.

In the nineteenth century, the army operated with a perspective that the needs of individuals, including wives and children, were subordinate to regimental interests. Until 1867 only six percent of soldiers could marry and bring their wives into barracks. Such wives were classed as 'married on strength' and it was only those wives who received any army recognition or entitlements. In 1867 new regulations were introduced about who could marry. These were: all warrant

officers, sixty percent of other sergeants and seven percent of lower ranks. Th
rules for officers were oral rather than written: 'subalterns must not marry
captains may marry; majors should marry; colonels must marry'. Over a hundre
years later it seemed to me that the unwritten rules for officers were pretty muc
still in place.

Throughout the twentieth century, the percentage of married personnel ha
grown steadily, eventually reaching the state where the military had become
society in which the majority of its members were married. Although the army
now had a very large number of wives and therefore children, old values an
structures did take a long time to change, and many of the 'old ways' were sti
evident during my regular service. Change was in the air, however, and th
presence of an increasing number of women and children, who brought civilia
attitudes and values of the wider society into the military community, in du
course led the army to take action.

In 1974, the Army Board commissioned the Army Welfare Inquiry and thi
was followed up a decade later by The Army Wives Study. This latter report
known as The Gaffney Report after Colonel and Mrs Gaffney who were aske
by the adjutant-general to 'determine those aspects of army life which caus
problems and aggravations for wives, and to recommend changes in the area
identified'. The process of change of course continues. One writer described th
journey as 'Transforming Wives into Spouses'.

We really didn't see all that much change in Scottish battalions between 197
and 1993. They were still very much communities in which the officers' wive
were the matriarchs of the battalion and expected to extend motherly care ove
the junior ranks' wives. There was often as much rank awareness among th
wives as among their men. Warrant officers' wives would be frowned upon i
they were too friendly with the wife of a private soldier. Officers' childre
disappeared off to prep school at the age of eight, returning home for schoo
holidays. Officers' wives were expected to be available to support the family o
the unit at the drop of a hat, and very few were in employment.

Christine and I fitted in pretty well with what was expected. We were
regarded as a little rebellious when we chose to send Barbara to a German
kindergarten in Osnabruck until she was old enough to attend the military
primary school. I suspect that hearing one of the soldiers' wives, who worked as
an army nursery assistant, saying that she had been 'learning the bairns their
ABCs', was what prompted us to look elsewhere. We found a delightful

indergarten where the children drank their hot chocolate from china cups. (It is mazing what catches your attention!) We were, however, just beginning to feel 1at we had made a dreadful mistake when Barbara, a very talkative child most f the time, broke her six-week silence at the kindergarten and started ommunicating in fluent German. She had clearly been saving herself until she ould make complete sentences.

That 'little rebellious' phase was to become a 'very rebellious' stage ten ears later when we took the children out of UK boarding school and home-chooled them in Germany. It was normal for officers' children to be sent off to rep school at the age of eight. Christine and I now look at our grandchildren and vonder how on earth we managed to send our own children off at such an early ge. But everyone else on the officers' patch was doing it, the children saw all 1eir friends going off, and anyone who didn't go would have been left alone on street with no other children their age. Personally, I don't think going off to chool so young ever seemed an issue to me. My own disrupted early childhood icluded a year or so in an orphanage as a seven-year-old. I was probably a bit esensitised to it all.

After looking at a variety of boarding schools situated sufficiently near the hildren's grandparents to make pick-up for exeats and half-term holidays easonably easy, we selected Cargilfield Preparatory School in Edinburgh. I guess that Barbara winning the military scholarship competition played a leciding part in our decision. (She had beaten a future Scots Guards officer, who secame RMA Sandhurst Adjutant, for the top prize.)

The whole boarding school package was made possible by the generous soarding school allowance which the MOD paid. This covered most of the soarding fees but fell short of meeting the 'extras' bill which seemed to grow erm by term as the children became more confident and more enthusiastic about ll sorts of additional activities. It was some years later that I discovered that the arge 'skiing' entry on the extras account was down to the children being asked in many Sunday mornings whether they would prefer to attend church or to go skiing at the dry ski slope at Hillend on the outskirts of Edinburgh. A small offering in the church collection plate would have been much cheaper for mum and dad than a ticket for the ski slope, but no one ever asked us.

The children did pretty well at boarding school and would have completed :heir whole school careers at private school had we not decided to leave the army and head off to America. We informed the children and the school of our

intentions, and when they flew to Berlin for their summer holidays in 1989, w
instructed them to leave their uniforms behind in the school second-hand shop

We didn't actually leave the army that year and I ended up soldiering on fc
another four years. Although I had accepted a posting to the Royal Scots in Wer
in West Germany, we decided to follow through on what we had been plannin
to do if we had gone 'across the pond', and confirmed that we would home
school the children. It was all a bit of an adventure for the children, and perhap
even at times for Christine and myself, but was verging on madness in the eye
of the army community. I am glad we did it, but there were days when we als
questioned our sanity.

Our house in the Buderich area of Werl near Dortmund, was a fairly moder
German house with a three-room cellar, in which we made a classroom with o
school desks and set about creating our school. The plan was that I would teac
maths and science before going off to work, and Christine would cove
everything else, using texts books which followed a set American curriculum
The BFES inspector came to check up on us. The unavoidable tension wa
broken early on when she made the mistake of accepting, along with a cup o
tea, the Berliner jam doughnut offered by one of the children. As she bit into it
the red jam filling spurted out all over her lovely white blouse. It is hard to b
severe and critical with four children aged 6, 8, 10 and 12, and their parents
when you have a huge red splodge on your previously immaculate outfit.

The Berliner provided us with a perfect object lesson for a history session o
JFK's 'Ich bin ein Berliner' speech... and we passed the inspection. Though
don't think the inspector was especially impressed by Christine's mnemonic fo
diarrhoea: 'disgusting insects and revolting rodents have open ended anuses' bu
it did work, and they can still spell it.

Over the 16 years of my regular army service we had nine homes and si>
international moves. If our first international removal from Inverness te
Osnabruck was traumatic, the next was even more so. We moved with three
children to Germany, and then from there with four to Hong Kong. We used to
joke that for a long time we believed that babies came with posting orders, bu
eventually discovered where they were coming from. Number four was Grahan
who was born in the British Military Hospital, Munster.

I had never been very good at attending births. Too much shouting and
emotion for me. I had taken Christine down to Munster the previous day. Sh
was overdue and about to be induced. We thought everything was about to

appen there and then, but the sister informed us that as the doctor wasn't present that Christine would 'just have to wait until the next day'. It was decided that she hould just stay in overnight, and I was sent home to look after the other three hildren. When Graham was born at five o'clock in the morning, without me resent, the nurse asked, "Would you like me to phone your husband, ma'am?" Christine replied that it would be better to leave it until after breakfast. What a tar!

So, we now had a fourth child and yet another posting order. We also had the official document required for Graham's birth to be registered as a UK citizen and resident, despite having been born in Germany. The form was addressed to he commanding officer 1 KOSB, who as 'father of the Battalion' was esponsible for making sure that we all carried out the correct registration of birth procedures. The official document from the doctor to the CO informed him that:

Mrs Christine A Blakey,
Wife of Captain Stephen A Blakey 504310,
has been delivered of a live,
male child on 13th May 1982.

The words 'live' and 'male' were typed beside 'stillborn' and 'female' respectively, so that the doctor just needed to score out the words which did not apply. The arrival of babies was clearly just one more element requiring efficient military processing.

Graham was our fourth and final child. We did keep receiving posting orders, but they didn't come with children in the future. For the next eleven years we took our four children to Hong Kong, then to Pirbright in Surrey, then to West Berlin, and to Werl in West Germany and then, on my final posting, to Inverness. We spent an average of two years in each location, and I think they all got used to having 'itchy feet' as the two-year stage approached, and we began planning for the next move. Malcolm lives in New Zealand now, and as I write is about to move into a new home with his wife Meron and their two children Ollie and Zahra. He is fully aware that he has picked up the habit of moving every two years.

The frequent moves, especially the international ones, meant that we didn't always have a car. What do you do, for example, when you arrive in Hong Kong knowing that you have less than 24 months before moving on to another country?

I had my own military vehicle for work, and public transport was pretty good but getting around with four children wasn't easy. We stalled in making decision until the commanding officer intervened.

Late one Friday afternoon, the telephone rang in our quarter, a lovely apartment in Repulse Bay with astonishingly beautiful views out over the South China Sea. It was the assistant adjutant of my unit, 1st Battalion Scots Guards. "Padre, the CO would like to see you on Monday morning."

I tried to explain that Monday was the padre's day off, and I had hoped to spend the day with my family. Mikie repeated the request, "10:00 hours Monday, Padre!"

"So, will that be in uniform?" I asked, thinking I could just drop up quickly to Stanley Fort, see the boss, and then head off out again. "Most definitely!" came the reply.

After a weekend wondering why the CO needed to see me, and in uniform, headed to work. My knock on the Orderly Room door was answered – "Come!" – and I marched in, approached the CO's desk and saluted. The CO was Lt Col Kim Ross. I suspect he was struggling to hide his amusement that his chaplain had been marched in to see him. I stood there, very aware that both the adjutant and assistant adjutant were sitting behind their desks watching and listening.

"Stephen, I have had a call from the defence auditor. He reported that he and his wife went shopping last week at the supermarket in Repulse Bay. As they were returning to their car, a black, army Mini parked beside them and an officer and his wife and four small children got out of it and headed off into the shop. Do you have any idea who that might have been?"

There was not a lot to say really. The defence auditor was probably the worst person I could have parked next to while guilty of the misuse of my military transport. I blushed and stammered and was told to go away and buy a car, and report back by the end of the week. "Yes, sir," I responded before saluting and exiting the Orderly Room with as much dignity as I could muster, but I swear that all three of the men sitting behind their desks were struggling to stifle a laugh as I marched out.

I did as ordered by the CO. My first Hong Kong car was a pretty dilapidated 12-year-old Saab 99 which had been passed from soldier to soldier over a number of years, and was showing signs of decay caused by a decade in a tropical climate. After six months it finally conked out one day when parked outside my church, St Barbara's Garrison Church in Stanley Fort. The church sat high up on promontory which overlooked the camp. The clapped-out car sat in the carpark outside the church for a few weeks while I decided how to dispose of it.

In the meantime, God was good, and we were offered a second-hand car which was being sold at a very reasonable price by a missionary who had completed his time in Hong Kong and wanted a quick sale. It was so much better than the black army Mini in all sorts of ways, not least in that it had proper air conditioning rather than the small electric fan glued to the dashboard which the army had kindly fitted in the Mini.

And the Saab? Well, I wasn't the only member of the Battalion who was paying the price for buying a second-hand car only to discover that it was on its last legs. There were a number of cars parked around Stanley Fort which clearly weren't going anywhere under their own steam. The regimental sergeant major finally lost patience with his camp being turned into a scrap yard and issued an order that unless these broken-down vehicles were removed within a week then he would have them removed and sold for scrap.

Just as this was happening, I was about to head off to Brunei for a week-long trip to the British troops based there. The military chaplains' parish of Hong Kong included Nepal, Korea and Brunei, and most months one of us would fly out to visit one of these locations to conduct church services, take schools assemblies, and carry out some pastoral visits. My senior chaplain seemed to keep the Korean visits to himself, but I did manage two visits each to Nepal and Brunei.

Prior to my first visit to Nepal in January 1983, a message came through from the army camp in Dharan in East Nepal, 'Ref. Visit by Padre from Hong Kong next week. Request he brings haggis. Stop.'

The Scots Guards chef duly made a haggis for me to take with me, and I set off wondering how I was going to explain this to the customs staff. I flew from Hong Kong to Calcutta, and on to Kathmandu, where I collected my baggage and headed towards the large brown army tent that sufficed as the terminal building in those days. I needn't have worried. My status as a British army officer seemed sufficient to avoid any awkward questions and I was waved through to the waiting staff car. After a couple of days in the city I jumped on a flight to Dharan.

The camp was the eastern recruiting centre for potential Gurkha soldiers. It was a fully self-sufficient barracks with facilities for the Gurkha soldiers serving

in the recruiting depot, and for the British staff and their families, and include
a British Military Hospital and a primary school.

I was met by the butcher, an Army Catering Corps sergeant from Glasgow.
"We're the only two jocks in town, Padre. So, I'll do the *Immortal Memory* an
Tam O'Shanter, and you're down for the *Selkirk Grace* and *The Address to th
Haggis.*"

These are the four of the cornerstones of any Burns Supper, celebrating th
Scottish national bard Robert Burns. With the exception perhaps of the poen
Tam O'Shanter, no Burns Supper would be complete without them. The Selkirk
Grace is only four lines of poetry, but the poem 'To a Haggis' is quite long an
requires confidence and dramatic input... and learning it off by heart took up
most of the next two days.

We had a great night, complete with Gurkha pipers and imported whisky.
My rendition, although I say it myself, was pretty good, and set me up for repea
performances at many Burns Suppers in the years to come.

My first visit to Brunei, 'sans haggis', looked as if it would be quite
straightforward. I was going to visit, and minister to, the British troops and thei
families who were supporting the Gurkha battalion based there, and also those
working with the Sultan's military. This visit was just a repeat of the routine
visits carried out by the Hong Kong based chaplains every second month. There
was the additional attraction that a company of the Scots Guards were on exercise
nearby and I would have the opportunity of visiting them at the Jungle Warfare
Camp.

The normality of the visit began to fade when warnings of a tropical storm
started to be broadcast. As I drove to Kai Tak Airport to catch my flight, I listened
on the car radio as the severe weather warning increased in severity and the
population was instructed to prepare for a typhoon. I flew out on one of the last
flights before the storm hit, not knowing what to expect on my return.

Four days later I landed back in Hong Kong and stared with shock as the
driver took me back home. The severe storm damage was everywhere to be seen.
Most dramatic of all were the ships sitting along the coast up above the high-
water line.

Christine and the children recounted how they had followed instructions,
bedded themselves down away from any windows in the bedroom corridor, and
sat out the storm. Our Filipino amah, Corina, had disappeared off somewhere
safe with all the other servants from our military accommodation block. The

mily had been terrified, but were safe, and later on we went out to explore the amage in the local area.

It was one of those times when I made the mistake of responding to the count of how difficult things had been with the words, 'Well, I'm home now!'

Over the sixteen years of my regular army service, and then a couple of times hen a reservist, Christine has been left in charge, carrying the can, looking after e children and the finances and the worries... and expected to be a good fficer's wife by caring for other families as well. Our times of separation cluded three tours of duty in Northern Ireland, exercises and operations in elize, USA, Italy, Nepal, Brunei, the Foot and Mouth epidemic, two Firemen's trikes, the First Gulf War, seven months in the Balkans... and a rugby tour back ome, plus at least one week-long residential chaplains conference each year.

During all of these periods when I was away from home on duty, the family as left to fend for itself. Fifty percent of the time they were based overseas, way from the support of any extended family, and dependent upon the military ystem.

It is often said that it is the wives who deserve the medals. The wives and the hildren too. Mine certainly do.

Oh, and the Saab 99? After Typhoon Ellen had calmed down a bit, the ommanding officer had phoned Christine. He was distraught by the damage to ur church, and wanted Christine to come and have a look. The CO's driver icked up Christine and drove her into camp, where Colonel Kim met her. The hurch really was a mess, the huge front door was off its hinges, there were rayer books floating down the flooded aisle, and the walls of the vestry were tripped bare of my various photographs and diplomas. "We'll get some soldiers n to sort it out before Stephen gets back from Brunei," he promised, but hristine was even more concerned that the Saab had been swept off the cliff by he storm.

Shame really, because we might have got some insurance money for it had he RSM and his team not had it removed a couple of days previously.

Chapter 9
Convergence and All Souls Ministry

"They always say time changes things, but you actually have to change them yourself." — Andy Warhol

'As an organisation the army has an obligation to care for its people, and the care must encompass every aspect of life – physical, mental, spiritual, medical, financial, dental...' It is a long list, and the spiritual dynamic is right in there along with all the others.

Over my forty years as an army chaplain I have seen the Royal Army Chaplains' Department, an organisation which informally, at least, describes itself as existing 'to make and sustain Christians', move down the path of process called 'convergence', to embrace 'all souls ministry' and to recognise that 'world faith chaplaincy' has to be part of fulfilling our role of looking after the spiritual and moral welfare of all of our troops and their dependants.

The 'duty of care' is of course balanced by the quid pro quo, that if we look after our personnel well, then they will function more effectively. His statement that 'an army marches on its stomach' reflects part of the great military understanding of Napoleon Bonaparte. He could have said that he had a duty of care to make sure that his soldiers were well fed, or he could have said that a hungry soldier is not going to fight very well. A good commander will ensure that his troops are well fed, and that every other aspect of their personal welfare is also well catered for.

In any project the bottom line is the outcome, and those involved with the planning and development of the project need to keep in mind the desired outcome. In the military, that goal is a well-honed, effective and flexible fighting force. Soldiers who are healthy and well supported in their private lives make for a good army. Those charged with the spiritual and moral health and support of he troops are, like every other agency, unavoidably involved in the process. haplains are not excused from serving their military masters, even if they regard erving God as a higher calling. The MOD does not employ chaplains to make oldiers into better Christians, it employs chaplains to help care for soldiers so hat they will contribute more effectively to the challenges of military life, ncluding killing the enemy.

After a short break at the end of my regular service, I re-enlisted as a reservist ınd attended my first Continuing Professional Development Course at the new Armed Forces Chaplaincy Centre at Amport House near Andover. The house 1ad previously been the home of RAF chaplaincy, and then later they shared it vith Royal Navy chaplains, before the army chaplains also moved in, and in nany ways took over due to our larger numbers.

During one of the sessions, the relationship between individual chaplains and ɔur army masters was being discussed. Never known as a good debater, I made he mistake of contributing to the discussion blurting out with something like, 'If the MOD didn't think that having padres would make the army a more ɔffective killing machine, they would get rid of us tomorrow!" That is not quite 1ow I would put it in a calmer moment, but there is some truth in that statement. (I was reminded of that recently by someone who I wasn't even aware was in the room at the time.)

There is no doubt that many of the influences for change in army chaplaincy match parallel causes of change in the rest of the society. The military is bound to reflect the society from which it draws its people, and as the profile and performance of the church has changed and reduced dramatically over recent decades in the civilian world, so it has also changed for those in uniform. Despite that, the profile of chaplains, and the value placed on them by those in authority, has been maintained at a high level.

Much has changed but many aspects of life have stayed the same, and I am convinced that one of the important constants in life is people and the human character. During padre's hours in Redford Barracks in the late 70s I would often develop a discussion among the jocks about belief, using definitions of theism, atheism and agnosticism as an easy way for each individual to explore where they themselves sat in terms of faith. Theists believe in a god or gods but cannot prove their view. Atheists believe that there are no gods but also cannot prove their position. Agnostics don't know or aren't sure, and perhaps sometimes don't really care.

After an often-lively discussion unpacking these three different approache
to belief in God we would have a show of hands, and invariably the voting woul
come out near enough to 25% theists, 50% agnostics and 25% atheists.

What has surprised me most is that those percentages have not changed ove
40 years. Most recently I was conducting my 'personal spiritual research' witl
recruits to the army reserve during their initial training, so this was men an
women 18–25 years old, coming straight out of civvy street. The raw materia
chaplains are given to work with, it seems to me, is much the same as when
joined up.

In 1985 I was sitting in the lecture room at Bagshot Park with a group o
Church of Scotland chaplains when the Deputy Chaplain General, Rev Jin
Harkness dropped by to share some dramatic news. He introduced hi
announcement with that well used saying, "I have some good news and som
bad news."

The good news was that the 'glass ceiling' on Church of Scotland chaplains
appointments, which meant that none of us could ever become chaplain general
had been broken, and that Jim himself would be the next chaplain general whe
Venerable Frank Johnston retired. This was indeed good news and meant tha
we now had parity with our Church of England colleagues.

The bad news was that we would lose some of the privileges we enjoyed a
ministers of the Kirk serving in the army, and that, for example, appointments
which we had always treasured as only ever being able to be filled by the Church
of Scotland would now be open to whoever was available at the time they became
vacant, whatever denomination the chaplain came from.

This downside to Jim's announcement was at that time only partially true.
His appointment did go a long way to creating parity across the department in
many ways, but at that stage this did not include the Roman Catholic chaplains.
It would take some more years and some pressure from higher up the military
chain of command before that changed.

Rev Jim Harkness, a Church of Scotland minister, served as chaplain general
1987–1995, and he was a good man to have in the chair at MOD Chaplains
(Army) during some years of interesting change and challenges for us all. With
the mould broken, the post of CG has now been filled over the past thirty years
by an Irish Presbyterian (Dobbin), a Methodist (Wilkes), a Baptist (Woodhouse)
and another Church of Scotland (Coulter) and three Anglicans (Blackburn and

Robbins and now Langston). At the time of writing there has yet to be a Roman Catholic chaplain general, but that day will come.

The army is forever in a state of flux, seeking to reshape itself in order to be increasingly 'fit for purpose'. History and traditions are important to military people, who are incredibly proud of the past, but there is always a danger of the old way of doing things becoming a barrier to future developments and improvements. It was by way of trying to ensure that the army was a sleeker, slimmer, more effective organisation that the Adjutant General's Corps was formed on 1 April 1992 with the aim of streamlining the management of the army's most precious resource, its personnel.

The plan was that the Corps would absorb the functions of six existing smaller corps; the Royal Military Police, the Royal Army Pay Corps, the Royal Army Educational Corps, the Royal Army Chaplains' Department, the Army Legal Corps and the Military Provost Staff Corps.

The plans for all of this were well advanced when they were sent to the chaplain general for comment. Rev Jim Harkness received the paperwork on return from an overseas trip and was given less than twenty-four hours to respond. He annotated the report and passed it to his Deputy Chaplain General, Rev Graham Roblin, for a full response to be prepared.

From a purely administrative perspective the idea that the RAChD should be absorbed into the new AG Corps did sound attractive, but the proposal was built on the false assumption that the relationship between chaplains and the army was the same as that experienced by lawyers, military police, educators and pay staff. The reality is that while chaplains serve in uniform and under military disciple and command, they continue to have a strong accountable relationship with their own denomination or 'Sending Church'. It is the Sending Church which authorises them to exercise their ministry, the Ministry of Word and Sacrament, and this external relationship differentiates them from everyone else in the army. This difference would be recognised some years later in Brigadier McGill's *Spiritual Needs Study*.

The response delivered by Rev Jim Harkness and Rev Graham Roblin was successful and the RAChD was left out of the plan for the new Adjutant General's Corps which was organised into four branches, Staff and Personnel Support (SPS), Provost (PRP), Educational and Training Services (ETS) and Army Legal Services (ALS).

The Department had won an important battle and maintained it individuality, but the on-going challenge of how to respond to an ever-changing military and civilian world continued. Some of the pressure to change came from within the MOD which of course was paying for chaplains and needed to know that it was getting value for money, and that the system was 'fit for purpose'.

In 1999 Brig IDT McGill, Late Royal Engineers, published An Investigation into the Need for Spiritual Values in the army. The McGill report on the *Spiritual Needs of the Army* was a hugely encouraging report for RAChD but it was also a challenging one.

McGill notes:

(Chaplains) are welcomed into the army while also answerable outside. This gives them unique independence: they are not part of the chain of command; they may hear what is confidential and are not obliged to report it; they have freedom to preach and reprove and encourage. The independence is important because the chaplaincy can provide a transcendent reference for the army's behaviour and a form of external scrutiny.

This succinct explanation shows just how impractical it would have been to include RAChD in the Adjutant General's Corps. The independence was, of course, not uncontrolled. chaplains have an important accountability to their own denomination.

McGill reaffirmed the commonly held view among chaplains that every major deployable army unit should have its own unit chaplain. This was over and above the number of chaplains required to cover all the training depots, garrisons and headquarters, and resulted in a recommended increase in the number of chaplains by fifty.

The McGill report also produced the imperative for the department to become much more unified. There was a quid pro quo. The Roman Catholics would join the unified department giving up some of their independence, and in exchange RC chaplains would be eligible for posts on the same basis as other chaplains i.e., best person for the job. There were some exceptions, of course, which were intended to ensure, for example, that the Roman Catholic Garrison Church in Aldershot would have a Roman Catholic chaplain, and not a minister from another denomination.

This process was called 'convergence' and it presented a considerable change across the department. The Church of Scotland chaplains had already accepted that they lost some of their individualism when Rev Jim Harkness became chaplain general, but the Roman Catholic chaplains still maintained their independence in all sorts of ways. RC Clergy were mainly based in Garrison Churches. Very few units would have a Roman Catholic chaplain. The exception would be units like the Irish Guards.

McGill's suggestion, which was actually soon taken as much stronger than just a 'suggestion', was that all of this needed to go. As army chaplains, and as Christian ministers, we should all be on a par, and whichever chaplain was on the ground at the time of spiritual need should respond to that need. There was a degree of fear and suspicion and resistance for some time, and a few awkward moments between chaplains of different denominations, but the issues were worked through, and a whole new working relationship was created. We were under command so to do.

Every chaplain was encouraged to understand that we had joined the army to minister to soldiers rather than to promote our own branch of Christianity. Chaplaincy is about the troops and their spiritual and moral welfare. We were called to minister to all souls.

The concept of 'all souls ministry' became important across the RAChD. Whichever chaplain was available at the time pastoral ministry was required would provide the support. The chaplain in a unit or garrison was chaplain to everyone, military and dependants, with no differential based on denomination, belief and creed. The chaplain is there for everyone, whether the person believes, or does not believe, in God.

This was in reality how most of us were already functioning as chaplains on the ground. Clearly there were issues when it came to the sacramental offices of Baptism, Confession and Holy Communion, but in my experience, soldiers were never much concerned about the denomination of the padre. Any resistance came from the clergy themselves.

The effect of convergence is clearly seen in the chaplains' posting plot. When I joined in 1977 there were six regular army chaplains based in Scotland. They were all Church of Scotland ministers and the idea that any of these posts would ever be filled by someone from outside the Kirk would have raised a laugh.

Over the intervening years the senior post in Scotland has been held by a Baptist minister, a Church of England clergyman and a Roman Catholic priest.

The present establishment of Regulars in Scotland is still six, and at the moment this includes a Methodist and a Baptist serving as unit chaplains. It is perhaps worth commenting that another of the unexpected changes in recent years is that at the time of writing there is an English Infantry Battalion based in Dreghorn Barracks, Edinburgh. And perhaps even more surprising is the fact that they have a Church of Scotland chaplain.

A bigger challenge for the military community was probably the changes in British society's attitude to human sexuality. These changes have taken longer to permeate the military community than many civilian sections of our nation but in due course their impact took hold, and in 2000 the official MOD policy changed to allow homosexual, lesbian and transgender personnel to serve openly in the Services.

It is difficult now for us to look back and to recall just what a huge paradigm shift this change of policy was. Like many other folks in the military I was very confused about what it all meant and unsure how on earth it would work itself out in practise. To help me understand, I volunteered to attend the Equal Opportunities Advisor Course at the Tri Service Equal Opportunities Training Centre at Shrivenham.

They were a very demanding few days. The issues were thrown at us and our prejudices were exposed. There was plenty of freedom to express our concerns and objections, but every statement was questioned and each of our personal views had to be justified. I did struggle with much of it but being free to share my concerns with others in a safe place over a gin and tonic or two in the evening was especially beneficial.

On the final day of the five-day course, we all took part in role play exercises. In my group role play I was cast as the grumpy, old major, single and living in the officers' mess and doing my best to maintain the 'good old standards and values'. I was warmly congratulated on my thespian skills by the other course members. "Well done, Padre, you really played that part well." The truth was that I really didn't need to act very much. I was simply being myself and portraying the society I had grown up in. It was very easy part for me to play and I clearly had an awful lot to learn, and quite a few prejudices that needed addressed, and views that could no longer be expressed.

It is always useful when chaplains take part in this kind of course. It exposes chaplains to the army, and the army to the chaplains. The chaplains' department has often run its affairs in its own way, usually slightly different from the rest of the army. These differences have sometimes helped to reinforce our individualism, our 'one foot in the system, and one foot out' status, but sometimes they have made chaplains look less than professional, and not at all in tune with the operating standards of the rest of the military. But the department has addressed many of these concerns and has continued to change.

The process through which I was accepted as an officer into the Royal Army Chaplain Department was very different from that experienced by other army officers. Everyone else had to attend go through the AOSB (Army Officers' Selection Board) system which had its roots in the War Office Selection Boards (WOSBs) of World War II. The WOSBs were created by army psychiatrists and established in 1942. They involved candidates taking a three-day stay in a country house, where tests were administered including written tests of mental ability, questionnaires, Leaderless Group tests and interviews. Psychiatrists and some psychological components of the WOSBs were removed from the Boards after the war. The Army Officer Selection Board was for a time known as the Regular Commissions Board (RCB).

Nowadays all potential chaplains have to attend an AOSB, presided over by the chaplain general, but which includes non-chaplains on the board. Not only is this a fairer, and hopefully more effective, way of selecting potential chaplains, but it also lets the rest of the army see that we are 'doing things properly'.

In addition to the changes in our selection process, which are designed to bring it more in keeping with the rest of the army, the career management of chaplains has also been brought in line. Postings are no longer determined by how the DCG's office cleaner rearranges the name tags on the wall after the wind has blown them all onto the floor. In 2014 RAChD Career Management was transferred from MOD Chaplains (Army) to the Army Personnel Centre (APC) in Kentigern House, Glasgow, developing what the then CG described as a 'fair, timely, responsive and accountable Career Management System'.

The 'old boy' network for joining the chaplains' department and for securing your next posting had gone. I guess that is a good thing.

Convergence and all-souls' ministry produced a more equal and united chaplain's department. Changes in selection and career management brought an increased professional edge to our working practices, bringing us more in line with the rest of the army. Equal opportunities policies and behaviour meant that chaplains learnt to relate to soldiers more equally whatever their sexuality or marital status. Perhaps the other major area which chaplains have had to address over these years has been how we relate to the members of other faiths and belief systems.

All three Armed Services have recruiting targets which are shaped by trying to ensure that the military community as far as possible reflects the ethnic, gender and religious profile of the nation. The picture of the very largely white, male Christian army which I joined in 1977 is a long way from this ideal. As the number of soldiers from other ethnic backgrounds and from other faiths has steadily increased, chaplains have had to adapt and change.

I think chaplains have always felt comfortable ministering to those of the Christian faith and to those of no faith. Many chaplains are much less at peace with the idea of being chaplain to those from another faith. Traditionally, the approach of the church to other faiths has been only of evangelism and conversion, with the aim of turning everyone into a Christian believer. But is that true chaplaincy?

Army chaplains are employed by the Ministry of Defence to look after the spiritual and moral welfare of the troops, by way of ensuring that the military system runs well, that the personnel are properly cared for, and that the army can do its job effectively. If a soldier from another faith, say Islam or Sikhism, is able to be a better soldier and to do his job to a higher standard because of his own faith, then the responsibility of his unit chaplain is surely to ensure that all reasonable facilities and support are put in place to allow for his or her spiritual growth. Proselytising is not an option despite the fact that it has been the traditional Christian approach.

This is a story which still has a long way to run. The army has had fulltime CCM's (Civilian Chaplains to the Military) since 2005 who are available to support military members of the Buddhist, Hindu, Jewish, Muslim, and Sikh faiths. The Equality Act of 2010 brought together a number of previous regulations and guidelines, and the military community has gone far in implementing the requirements in the same way as the civilian world. There is, however, still progress to be made in including World Faith Leaders as equals within the RAChD.

The department has changed in all sorts of ways which would have been unimaginable 40 years ago. Some of these I found easier to cope with than others, and throughout all of the adapting to this I had my own struggles to deal with.

Chapter 10
Spiritual Challenges

'Heaven is full of answers to questions which nobody ever bothered to ask." —
Rev Billy Graham

I had been with my first Battalion for about 15 months when my boss, Rev
Farquhar Lyall, ACG HQ Scotland (Army), phoned me one Monday morning.
'Stephen, I know it's your day off, but I need a quick chat. Can you come over
to the house after work, say 18:00 hours?"

I have never been very good at dealing with the gap between receiving a
summons and finding out the cause. My residual guilty conscience always
assumes that I have done something wrong, been found it, and that I am about to
get into trouble. I had, in fact, done nothing wrong this time. No one had done
anything wrong, but one of our colleagues had decided that the time had come
for him to leave army chaplaincy, and his departure was going to result in a
couple of us having to move postings at short notice.

One of the Irish Presbyterian army chaplains was leaving the RAChD
because he felt that he was in danger of 'losing his soul'. I never did manage to
ask him about his concerns, though looking back I should probably have done
so. I am sure that he was struggling to work through feelings of compromise
which are probably experienced by most army chaplains from time to time.

He had just recently been informed of his next posting, which was to a unit
about to be deployed to Belfast on Operation BANNER. The timing of his
leaving the army would have meant that he would be in Belfast with the British
army during the months when he was applying for a parish in Northern Ireland.
It was felt that this was unfair due the sensitive political situation in the Province,
and that some other chaplain should cover this unit.

Christine and I had just put in an offer to buy a house in Edinburgh, with the expectation that I would be remaining at Redford Barracks for another two year. I did try to explain this to Farquhar, but he made some comment about 'being in the army now' and informed me that I was expected in Fort George, Inverness in four weeks' time, ready to start Northern Ireland training with 1st Battalion King's Own Scottish Borderers.

Army chaplaincy involves holding in balance a range of different, and sometimes conflicting, values and priorities. You find yourself serving three masters, well at least three masters: the army; the church (as represented by your own denomination); and Almighty God. There is often tension between the expectations and demands of these three masters, and that tension can really only be worked out individually by each chaplain. There is always the temptation to just ignore the tensions and hope that in time they will go away, but most of the issues have to be addressed eventually.

When I was born my mother and her husband were living apart. He was quite sure that I was not his child and insisted that he would only take my mother back if she get rid of me. So I was fostered informally for my first four years until my birth-mother gave up trying to persuade her husband to accept me into the marital home. At that stage it was then decided that I should be put up for adoption, and so I was then legally fostered for a couple of years, before spending some time in an orphanage and then, at the age of eight, being adopted into the Blakey family. This all left me with a pretty relaxed, and sometimes almost irresponsible, attitude to life.

I have certainly had a tendency to 'go with the flow' and have not always been good at thinking through the second consequence of my actions, and a strong tendency to live in the short term. When spiritual or practical influences come into conflict, I have, in the past, too easily ignored the long-term outcome and just got on with what needed to be done that day or followed the path of least resistance with the best benefits available there and then.

I should point out that I have never regarded myself as having had an unhappy childhood. The uncertainty and variety of life was all that I knew, and I learnt early how to adapt to whatever setting I found myself in. I was, however pretty confused when, at the age of seven, I was told that my birthday was 5 July The previous year we had celebrated it on 3 August.

Becoming a member of the Blakey family brought me into evangelical Christian circles, and I became a Christian about the age of twelve at a Scripture nion holiday camp. My spiritual convictions matured during my secondary hool years, but it did sometimes look as if my spiritual life and my non-spiritual fe were developing on two very different planes. These two planes didn't meet p or impact each other very often at all, and people would sometimes challenge le about this. I certainly was not practising what I preached, or living out what said I believed in.

I did have a growing conviction that God had been really good to me iroughout my early years. I identified his goodness toward me in my salvation, le quality of life I enjoyed, and the family into which I had been adopted. My fe could all too easily have turned out to be very different. I really appreciated rowing up in St Andrews, and the ease with which I seemed to drift through life nd education added to a strong belief in God's goodness, and a deep sense of ratitude led me to want to repay God for all his generosity towards me. In my iind the most obvious way to do this was to become a clergyman. The Blakeys rere a Church of Scotland family, and so it seemed to make sense that the iinistry of the Kirk was for me. It may sound very simple and straightforward, nd perhaps even naive, but that was where my call to Christian ministry came :om.

It would be fascinating to do some research into why other people have hosen the clergy career path. When I was reading theology at New College, dinburgh I would sometimes look around the common room at what seemed to le to be a peculiar collection of slightly strange folk who had responded to a call' to become the spiritual leaders of our nation. "God," I would ask, "what's o strange about me, that I fit in with this odd crowd of folk gathered here?" I on't think I ever got an answer.

In those days the path towards ordination for most prospective Church of cotland parish ministers involved firstly taking a non-theological degree. During the three or four years of that degree you would apply to be considered s a candidate for the ministry, and attend a weekend long residential Selection chool. If accepted as a candidate, you would then, on completion of your first legree, study for a Bachelor of Divinity degree at one of the historic Scottish niversities. (St Andrews, Edinburgh, Glasgow or Aberdeen.)

I started off my tertiary education at St Andrews University studying Pure Maths, Applied Maths and Statistics (though within a few weeks I replaced tatistics with Physics), and early in my second year I filled out the application orm for the Church of Scotland Ministry. On the Sunday evening when I was intending to post my application form, I was on my way to St Andrews Bapti Church to witness the baptism of one of my old school friends, when anoth friend driving past offered me a lift to church, and so the envelope with th application form was still in my pocket at the end of the service.

That service was my first experience of adult baptism by immersion. included a powerful and emotional sermon on the importance of believer baptism (as opposed to infant baptism). The whole event left me confused abor the theology of baptism, so much so that it was a couple of weeks before decided to go ahead and post that application form. While I still had questions i my mind about infant baptism versus believers' baptism, I reasoned that it wa God who had got me into the Church of Scotland fold, so He must either have plan for me in the Kirk or He could just as easily shut the door.

God didn't shut the door, and my progress through the various challenge and requirements to achieve ordination went smoothly. I was still living two live – the spiritual Christian with a call on his life and the beer drinking, rugb playing, rogue – and I seemed to manage to get away with it fairly well. An because I got away with it, it became the pattern of much of my life.

* * * * *

It was my army chaplaincy colleague's fear that he was in danger of losin his soul that resulted in my posting to Fort George, 13 miles west of Invernes in the north of Scotland in 1979. I had expected to serve a much longer time i Edinburgh and had actually been told that I would remain in Redford Barrack to take over as padre of The Royal Scots when they moved back from Munste in Germany later in 1979. Instead I was given four weeks to move to the King Own Scottish Borderers at the Fort.

By this time I had been in the army for long enough to begin to feel prett confident that I had made the correct decision in joining up, and that my futur lay in this form of ministry. I was enjoying army life, both the work and th social aspects, and the army seemed to like me. I fitted in well and could see n reason why this wouldn't be my home for many years to come.

My assurance was soon to be shaken, however, when I found myself som weeks later reflecting on how I was actually spending my days. It was all a bi of a rude awakening. I had just been to visit a young soldier in the guard room He had some issues with his family back home in Lanarkshire and, not knowing low else to help them, he had gone AWOL (absent without authorised leave) so he could spend time with them. When he eventually returned to the unit, he was charged with being absent and given a week's detention.

As was my habit, I dropped by the guardroom to visit the soldiers awaiting sentence and the soldiers under sentence. I chatted for a while with this particular soldier, and at the end of the day headed off home to Christine and the family in Inverness. My time in the cell with the Jock had left me unsettled. He appreciated my visit, but I knew that anyone else would have been just as welcome, and just as effective. I had done nothing spiritual for him. A social worker might have brought him more benefit. Was I really exercising a proper Christian ministry among my soldiers?

It was with this sense of unease playing on my mind that I caught the overnight sleeper train from Inverness to London to attend a Continuous Professional Development course at RAChD Centre at Bagshot Park. The focus of the three-day course was to train army chaplains in preparing and delivering radio talks. All chaplains were expected to take their turn in writing and delivering the daily 'God slot' for BFBS radio, and most of us were greatly in need of some professional training.

During these few days at Bagshot Park, my sense of unease was turned around. In a time of prayer with colleagues Padre Keith Crozer and Padre Patrick Springford, I experienced a spiritual refreshing. Some would call it being 'baptised with the Holy Spirit' or 'filled with the Holy Spirit', and I guess over the years I have described it in a number of different ways. Whatever words are used the result is the same. I had moved from feeling that I was spiritually dry and had little to offer my soldiers, to a conviction that God's love and grace was such that I had a much richer and fuller package of spiritual gifts to share with those God had called me to minister to.

It wasn't quite St Paul's Damascus Road experience, but it was certainly the start of a new journey, a journey which would bring me many challenges, as well as opportunities, as I sought to explore new areas of Christian living and ministry. I wasn't too sure what Christine would think of my newfound spirituality, so I telephoned her the night before I was due to travel back north to Inverness. "I've had an interesting spiritual experience," I tried to explain. I needn't have worried. When I got back home, she explained that she had been praying for me for ages, hoping that I would get back some of the spiritual spark which had attracted her to me when we first met years before.

Shortly after this experience we moved as a family to Osnabruck, where ther was a growing number of evangelical and charismatic Christians within th British community. Many had come to faith in lively churches back in the UK and were now looking for a similar church experience in Germany. The Charismatic Movement was in full swing back home, so it was not surprising that the military community was touched by this new expression of the Christian faith. Christine and I helped to bring together many folks who had been influenced by this movement, and we enjoyed great times of fellowship and teaching, which really did make it feel as if we were experiencing a serious move of God.

This period is reported in the RAChD Journal as follows:

The spiritual life of the chaplains in Osnabruck is greatly helped by regular Devotional Days which they take in turn to lead. This has proved to be a tremendous base from which to go out in ministry.

Chaplains' wives also started a regular meeting for prayer which has gradually grown with other committed Christian women joining. A church newspaper called 'Together' is produced monthly and is a very good organ for news and views on the church scene, and recently a Gospel Service has started on Sunday evenings, which encourages and gathers together people who might etherise find the traditional worship unhelpful.

During this time I read a book by a Hong Kong Missionary called Jackie Pullinger. Her book *Chasing the Dragon* had become a popular Christian best seller, and her remarkable story was well known. Jackie's ministry was very largely with drug addicts, often in an area known as the Walled City near Kai Tak Airport, in Kowloon. Many of the individuals she worked with became Christians and were set free from their addiction by the power of prayer. When it was confirmed that our next posting was to be Hong Kong, everyone encouraged us to connect with this remarkable lady.

I have now known Jackie for over 35 years, and I think she has only once personally answered the phone herself when I have called her home or office. Every other time an assistant or PA has answered, and then insisted on taking a message rather than 'putting me through'. Had Jackie not answered personally that first time I called, I might well have been put off trying again, but she did answer, and we talked, and in time we became good friends.

Throughout our two years with the Scots Guards in Hong Kong we spent quite a lot of our free time with Jackie. We attended the Saturday evening church meetings which she ran in Mid-Levels, Hong Kong, supported her missionary work, baptised a number of her ex-drug addict converts and enjoyed social times together like watching the Hong Kong International Rugby Sevens. My conviction that the Christian faith really only works properly when the Holy Spirit is fully expressed and experienced, continued to develop and mature. There seemed to be within me a growing separation between the formal organised religious form of Christianity which was suited to army chaplaincy and fitted well with 'serving the system' on the one hand, and my personal desire for a vibrant, powerful, spiritually effective faith on the other.

The move from Osnabruck to Hong Kong also provided a ready solution to a problem I had been living with for some considerable time. Our years in Osnabruck coincided with a period of heightened debate within the Church of Scotland regarding the Sacrament of Baptism, and whether individuals who had been baptised as babies could then have a second baptism as an adult believer. Church doctrine was very clear – An individual can only be baptised once – but many people who had a conversion experience really wanted to respond to the Biblical instruction to 'believe and be baptised'. There had been a number of instances of these 'second baptisms', and each time they had caused all sorts of ructions. It was a hot topic, and I was frequently asked, mainly by young evangelical soldiers, "So, Padre, were you baptised as a baby, or as a believer?"

It was a difficult question for me, as I hadn't been baptised at all, which was pretty unusual for a Church of Scotland ordained minister.

My first foster mother was a member of the Salvation Army, and she had arranged for me to be dedicated as a baby in the Salvation Army church in Dumfries. Although the Salvation Army is a church in all sorts of ways, it does not recognise any sacraments, such as baptism or communion, as essential parts of the faith. The SA does not teach that sacraments are wrong, but it believes that they are unnecessary, and may be unhelpful to some.

I was adopted into the Blakey family at the age of eight, and they also adopted a baby boy, Gordon, that same summer. When they were planning for Gordon to be baptised, the parish minister of Killermont Parish Church on the northside of Glasgow, Rev Jack, decided that there was no need for me to be baptised, as I had already been dedicated. I remember Gordon's baptism well, but I do not have any memory of the conversations leading up to my confirmation as a communicant member of the Church of Scotland as a 16-year-old, and so have no idea if anyone ever asked if I had been baptised.

The question first came into focus for me when I was serving a ministry student attachment in St Thomas's Junction Road Church in Leith during my second year of theology training. I was asked to remain behind after a Sunday morning service to witness the baptism of three adults. It did seem a bit strange to me that this was all happening in private rather than in the face of the congregation. I asked each of the three folk being baptised what had brought them to the decision to request baptism, and one of them said, "Well, I was brought up in the Salvation Army, and as they don't do baptism, I need to be baptised so I can join the Kirk."

You can imagine that this stirred some interest in me, and raised a number of questions, but I guess I reasoned that as I was by now a fully confirmed member of the Church of Scotland and well on my way to becoming an ordained minister... well, I'm not quite sure how my reasoning went but in the end, I decided to let sleeping dogs lie. All would be well (I hoped!).

Perhaps all would have been well had it not been for folk asking awkward questions and the problem of having to be creative in my answers.

In 1982, having left Osnabruck, we were staying in St Andrews for a few weeks before flying out to Hong Kong, and I was invited once again to attend a baptismal service in St Andrews Baptist Church. Memories of my previous experience there came to mind, and I got to thinking that this might be the perfect answer to my problem i.e., the problem of being the only unbaptised ordained minister in the Kirk.

With a surprising rush of common sense, which was probably stirred by my wife's timely advice, I decided to phone the then current senior army chaplain at headquarters (army) Scotland to ask his advice. Rev Eustace Annesley, assistant chaplain general at that time. He was a lovely gentle man and I felt he would listen sympathetically to my plight.

Having done my best to explain my un-baptised state, I said, "So, I thought as I am back in my hometown, that I might go along to the Baptist Church and get baptised on Sunday evening." There was a pregnant silence on the other end of the phone line...

"Stephen, where are you at the moment?"

"At my folk's house in St Andrews," I replied.

"Can you just stay there? Don't do anything just now. I'll call you back shortly."

Fifteen minutes later, Eustace called back. He had clearly taken advice elsewhere. "Stephen, here is what we would like you to do. You leave for Hong Kong next week. We suggest that you do nothing at the moment, that you stay away from St Andrews Baptist Church, and that once you are out in Hong Kong, you find somewhere where you can get baptised quietly. That would be the best thing to do."

For a change, I did as ask, and kept away from the Baptist Church that Sunday. Ten days later Christine and I and our four children flew to Hong Kong, and I promptly forgot all about the suggestion that I should find a quiet out-of-the-way location to remedy my unorthodox baptismal state.

That was until a couple of months later when Jackie Pullinger phoned up one Friday evening. "Stephen," she asked, "what is your view on believers' baptism?" The English Chamber Orchestra was on tour in Hong Kong at the time, and some of the members had attended one of Jackie's meetings on their night off. A number had accepted Jesus as Saviour and were keen to be baptised before flying home to UK. Jackie thought that it would be good if they could return to London saying that they had been baptised by a proper clergyman, and perhaps I could be that person.

Well, the conversation was long and interesting, and resulted in us agreeing that Jackie and some of her team would come and preach at St Barbara's Garrison Church in Stanley Fort on the following Sunday morning. After the church service a crowd of us made our way down to the beach beside the Stanley Services' Yacht Club, where Christine and I were baptised in the South China Sea by Jackie Pullinger and Su Ming, a recovered heroin addict. It was quite a remarkable day. Although I didn't baptise the members of the ECO I did have the honour of conducting the baptism of quite a number of new converts in the South China Sea over the next year or so, including Gogo, the former leader of the 14K Triad, who appeared in Jackie's book.

Baptising adult believers in the open air does have a lovely spiritual side to it. When I returned to Germany for a few months after the First Gulf War, and before the Royal Scots moved back to the UK, we held a Baptism Service in a nearby German lake. A number of our soldiers had come to faith on Operation GRANBY, as had some of the wives back in Werl, West Germany.

135

I think we had about a dozen cars driving in the convoy as we headed off the lake. We arrived at the Strandbad (bathing beach) to be told by the German Lifeguard that it was too cold to swim. In my best German I did my best to get him to change his mind, but this was Germany, where rules are meant to be kept. After some conversation he advised us that there was another beach further along the lake that was not controlled, and so we could do whatever we wanted along there.

It was numbingly cold in the water, but we had a wonderful celebration followed by a barbecue which warmed us all up.

During my time in Hong Kong, I resigned my commission, with a plan to stay to work with Jackie and her St Stephen's Society. Within a week I was back in the UK. Perhaps believing that the cool, green grass of home would calm my mind, I was summoned urgently to meet the chaplain general at Bagshot Park and then sent up to Edinburgh to meet Rev Jim Harkness, assistant chaplain general at HQ Scotland (army). They both talked through with me the implications of what I had announced, and then put me back on the flight to Hong Kong.

On returning to my family in the Far East there was much to think about, and big decisions to be made. In the end I didn't leave the department at that time, and nor did I leave five years later when Jim Harkness once again, this time as chaplain general, had the task of settling my mind against my intention to resign and encouraging me to serve on until the end of my commission. I didn't leave the army either time, but I didn't completely settle either, and I continued, and still continue, to struggle to hold in balance my formal Presbyterian ministry and my experience of, and hunger for, a deeper more powerful and dynamic spiritual life.

Perhaps by this time there were actually three competing personae struggling to control my life. The rugby playing, beer drinking character was still as strong as ever, but there were now two spiritual characters. One was structured and Presbyterian, and very much the army chaplain. The other was wildly charismatic and therefore less well suited to military church life and service.

Being spiritually radical tended to draw other like-minded, or perhaps 'like spirited', people to Christine and myself. We enjoy what some would describe as 'happy clappy' style worship, and people would often look to us to organise events. There were already a couple of well-established organisations for Christians in the military, but they tended to hold theological views which struggled with the whole Charismatic area. We were being encouraged to develop something which would meet this new hunger.

I have always been a strong advocate of not asking a question if you suspect that you might not like the answer, so rather than ask permission or authority to develop an organisation, Christine and I rounded up a group of army officers' wives and formed the Wives Renewal Network.

After running a couple day conferences it soon became clear that there were as many men as women involved, and so the Wives Renewal Network very soon morphed into the Forces Renewal Network which ran a number of very successful events and conferences in UK and in Germany. We produced teaching papers called *Anakainos Papers* on such topics as '*The Gift of Tongues*' and '*Being Filled with the Spirit*'.

Some of this was supported and even financed by the military authorities, but much of it was independently sponsored. The chaplains' department took care to sit alongside the various spiritual organisations, encouraging the spiritual life of officers and soldiers, but often holding back from officially endorsing the work. Forces Renewal Network was treated in very much the same way. FRN was permitted to use the RAChD Conference Centre, Church House Lubbecke for a house party, and an article entitled '*Evangelism in der Kraft des Geistes*'. (Evangelism in the Power of the Spirit) was included in the Royal Army Chaplains' Journal.

It was during all this time that I became increasingly involved with and connected to the Vineyard Christian Fellowship. It is still, in many ways, where my heart lies. The first leader of the Vineyard was John Wimber, who was manager of the Righteous Brothers when he became a Christian. At the time of his conversion their hit song 'You've lost that loving feeling' was in the top ten. He brought into the church a wonderful musical heritage which has influenced modern worship songs ever since.

Christine and I were introduced to the Vineyard Movement by Jackie Pullinger, and we used our overseas leave pass from Hong Kong to visit the church in Los Angeles. The church was located in Yorba Linda, not far from Disneyland. My less than supportive friends have remarked on the proximity from time to time. The combination of the ministry of Jackie Pullinger and the worship style and teaching of the Vineyard Ministries International have probably been the most profound influences on my personal spirituality and ministry. I have often been sure that my future lay in working fulltime in a setting which would allow these influences to blossom and to define the shape of my work, but this has never actually happened, and I remain thoroughly thrilled to the Kirk, and thereby living with a certain inner tension.

Part of that tension was always going to be unavoidable for me in a chaplaincy ministry. chaplaincy is always a challenge for those with an evangelical theology. The task of chaplaincy is really to serve whatever organisation you are chaplain to. You care for the spiritual and moral welfare of the personnel by way of enhancing the bottom line or achieving the goals of your employer. That bottom line will often shape your ministry just as much, if not more than, your concern for the eternal destiny of the people.

Being evangelical and having a desire to see all people make a personal spiritual commitment to the Christian faith, means that it is unavoidable to challenge individuals with the claims of Christ, and to encourage a response. I sometimes think it is a bit like asking someone to marry you. How often can you propose marriage to someone who turns you down? Does the relationship not just become really awkward? As a chaplain, in any organisation, how often can you challenge someone with the claims of the Christian faith, without them starting to avoid you? And so, the tension remains.

I left the regular army in 1993 with a clear plan to work with the Vineyard Christian Fellowship denomination. The Vineyard international leader, John Wimber, had given me authority to plant vineyard churches in Scotland, and I left RAChD full of hope and expectation. Things did not turn out the way we had hoped and within a year or so I found myself in a Church of Scotland parish church. Over the last 25 years, I have served in four different parishes, and in each place have struggled to find the right balance between my traditional parish ministry and my own personal spirituality. There has always been a tension, but perhaps Christian ministry needs a tension to keep it vibrant.

Chapter 11
The Four Fs

'Among the soldiers, the 'four Fs' were inevitably known as the 'eight Fs': 'fookin' floods', 'fookin' fuel', 'fookin' fires' and 'fookin' foot and mouth'." — *General Mike Jackson*

It happens so often that few of us are ever surprised when we see the troops mobilised to help our nation in an emergency situation. Flooding is probably the most common issue they are called out to help with, but there are others. This emergency response is known as Military Aid to the Civil Authorities (MACA) and is an important function for our Armed Forces. This includes Fire-Fighting, Foot and Mouth, Floods, Fuel, and perhaps there was also in my years in uniform a fifth F' – Flight Pan Am 103 – blown up over Lockerbie in 1988. This MACA function involves our troops being ready to provide practical support when our civil authorities are overwhelmed by the demands of an emergency situation. The armed forces provide this support from its spare capacity, and so the availability is dependent on the primary military demands having first been met.

During my military service the army has had to play its part all four of the 'four F's' though I personally have only been involved with two of them: Firefighting and Foot-and-Mouth.

My first experience of this came early on in my time with the Royal Highland Fusiliers, in November 1977, when firefighters launched their first national strike for a quarter of a century. Pay talks had broken down in anger, bitterness and suspicion, with more than 55,000 firemen abandoning their posts after their union leaders had rejected the pay offer which had been recommended by an independent review body.

I had only been with my unit for a few weeks when the strike began and I was still trying to get to grips with my role as an army chaplain. As soon as the

strike took effect the Battalion was deployed to Strathclyde to cover for th
striking firemen and, as their padre, my place was clearly with the troops.

I had inherited Corporal 'Mac' as the padre's driver from my predecesso
Cpl Mac in turn seemed to have inherited the padre's driver's ability of drivin
like a maniac and scaring the living daylights out of his boss. Over the next 1
years as a regular army chaplain I enjoyed the support of a good number c
drivers, who usually also fulfilled some batman and orderly duties. These othe
duties include such tasks as polishing the padre's boots, cleaning the office an
the church, running errands and looking after the car. Nothing too taxing.

It would take a whole other chapter, however, to recount all of the storie
about the surprises and the stress they each caused me. Soldiers were ofte
appointed as the padre's driver by way of either keeping them out of som
troublesome situation they had got involved in, or saving them from a mor
demanding role. None of them was ever going to rise up through the ranks. Th
misdemeanours were numerous: one of them got drunk on the Communio
Wine, one went absent, one borrowed my typewriter and, when it got damage
in a barrack room brawl, he buried it to try and get rid of the evidence, one wa
charged with driving on a road that was away from the authorised duty rout
(which he would have got away with had he not reversed into a German civilian'
BMW)... and then there was Rocky in Berlin.

Rocky, Lance Corporal Roxburgh, Black Watch, was a nervous sort at th
best of times. It wasn't helped when the other battalion MT (Motor Transport
platoon drivers informed him that he needed to carry two spare wheels when w
drove through Checkpoint Charlie into East Berlin. I don't know exactly how
many wheels we had with us that particular day, but I do know that he panicke
on our way back towards the West and turned down the wrong street in Eas
Berlin, where we met hundreds of Communist soldiers who were forming up fo
a parade. His panic mushroomed and he decided that acceleration was the
answer. He swerved round another corner and we found ourselves in the middl
of a parade square where May Day rehearsals were taking place. He left a lot o
rubber on the tarmac as we skidded our way round all four sides of the hollow
square of totally bemused Russian and East German soldiers. We avoided
causing an international incident, but I am sure there is a report in a folder dee
in a filing cabinet, somewhere in Berlin.

Back in 1977, as well as Cpl Mac, I had also inherited a 1972 Ford Escor
Estate, which had been sprayed white to make it incognito in Northern Ireland

It was passed on to whichever chaplain was deployed from Scotland to Northern Ireland on Op BANNER in the rather naive thought that it would be less obviously a military vehicle in the eyes of the Provisional IRA. Some would suggest that its strength was actually that it stood out amongst the other military pool cars as a chaplain's car and was therefore less likely to be targeted by the terrorists.

All chaplains were given a non-military vehicle for their own duty use. Because we were 'on call' 24/7 these vehicles were issued on a permanent basis and could be taken home and parked outside our married quarter overnight. There were strict rules about their use and about who could travel in them. The white Ford Escort was my first Padre's car.

The day after the Battalion deployed through to Strathclyde, Mac and I loaded up a large film projector and a couple of Services Sound and Vision Corporation (SSVC) 8mm films and headed off to visit my firefighting soldiers in Glasgow. There were no CD-ROMs in those days. I had picked up that this is what padres did – you visited the troops wherever they were, and if they had lots of spare time on their hands you could show them movies, supplied by SSVC. Soldiers almost always had time on their hands, soldiers lived and still live in a 'hurry up and wait' scenario.

It was the days before the city planners had torn a path through the middle of Glasgow for the M8 motorway, so driving through the city was a good bit slower than it is now. We were working our way along a busy rush-hour Alexandra Parade when a Green Goddess fire engine, lights flashing and siren blaring, appeared in the distance. Without so much as a 'What do you think, Padre?' Cpl Mac slammed his foot to the floor, and we were off in hot pursuit. "Shame we don't have one of these flashing lights like Kojak," he called out as he crossed the central white line to overtake a couple of cars.

The 'Green Goddess' fire engines were built between 1953 and 1956 for the Auxiliary Fire Service which had been was established as part of the UK's Civil Defence. It was thought that a nuclear attack on Britain would cause a large number of fires, which would overwhelm the ordinary fire service. These machines, which would be better described as self-propelled pumps were held in reserve until 2004 when they were disposed of.

Surprisingly (and I was often surprised when one of my drivers delivered me safely to the correct destination) we arrived at the factory from which smoke was pouring, and in front of which two 'Green Goddess' fire engines were disgorging

soldiers, who in turn were unloading hoses and ladders. The first hose was roll
out with great aplomb from its coiled-up storage shape into a long snake alor
the factory forecourt. A soldier grabbed the end nearest to the fire engine only
discover that he was trying to connect a male connector to another ma
connector. They would get better at all of this.

My attention was distracted by a guy with a microphone followed by anoth
with a TV camera approaching me with some enthusiasm. "Sir, this is the fir
incident the men have been called out to, would you like to…"

I didn't hear any more. Panic set in. I wasn't used to being called 'sir' b
anyone and quickly realised that I was the only officer on the scene and that m
nice new Captain's rank slides did make me look quite important. I backed o
around the back of the vehicle and removed my rank slides!

My face did appear on the BBC nine o'clock news that evening b
fortunately not in a speaking role, and no one ever picked me up for walkir
around with no badges of rank visible.

For Mac and I, the rest of the firefighting was much more controlled. Mo
of the time was spent receiving and distributing good-will gifts which wer
handed in by the good people of Glasgow, who greatly appreciated what th
troops were doing. I remember dropping into the Scripture Union Office in 28
St Vincent Street. I was in uniform and was given a warm reception by the offic
staff with whom I had often worked during my university vacations. The
handed over a large tin of Quality Street. I don't think we ever managed to sho
any films, but we did distribute lots of sweeties.

The soldiers did a great job as reflected in this account from the Glasgo
Evening Times:

*RHF troops were found in action on the streets of Glasgow. They rushed t
the rescue in Ardenlea Street, Dalmarnock, in November 1977 when a famil
was trapped in a blazing tenement. A tiny ledge 50ft up provided a hai
raising escape for two families trapped on the top floor after a gas lea
sparked a fire. At the height of the blaze resident Tommy Jamieson, trappe
with his wife and children, and another family on the top floor climbed acros
to the top window in the next close. Mr Jamieson smashed the window an
led his family and neighbours to safety.*
*No one was seriously injured in the fire, but more than 20 families were le
homeless.*

The soldiers were on the streets because firefighters were on strike, and,
helped by some of the strikers who had promised not to put lives at risk, they
helped rescue other families trapped in the middle flats by choking smoke.

The firefighters were on strike in an attempt to win a pay rise. In due course
hey were given a 10% increase, and returned to work. Then 25 years later, we
ound ourselves back in the same place, this time on Operation Fresco.

In November 2002 I was asked to take the morning service in my old church,
St Margaret's Garrison Church, Redford. By this time I was an army reserve
chaplain covering for one of my regular colleagues who was overseas on
operations. I introduced myself to the congregation with, "It is quite strange
being here today. 25 years ago, I was chaplain here in Redford and the troops
were engaged in firefighting."

As the congregation left the church after the service, one lady paused while
shaking my hand. "I too was here 25 years ago!" It was Betty Macdonald whose
husband had been Technical Quartermaster of 1 RHF back in 1977. Bob and
Betty were our first neighbours on an army patch (army married quarters estate).
Bob, like his boss QM Stevie Simpson were both actually Royal Scots but then
served together with 1 RHF on commissioning. They were my first QMs. One
of the invaluable pieces of advice given at my intake course at Bagshot Park was
to befriend the Quartermaster. And I had done this with Stevie and Bob.

General Mike Jackson reflected on firefighting in August 2002:

More than 30,000 British troops have been secretly ordered to be ready for
firefighting duties as concern mounts at the prospect of the first national
firemen's strike since 1977. All army headquarters in Britain were told last
week to begin planning for the strike, which is expected to take place from
October 26, as the nation's 50,000 firefighters pursue a pay increase of
almost 40 per cent.

The famous old Green Goddesses trundled out of their depots. Now retired
from service, these iconic vehicles had been procured for civil defence in the
1950s to be ready to put out fires after a Soviet nuclear attack on Britain.
But though by now very ancient, they still did a good job. The soldiers quite
enjoyed the firefighting, even if some might have been irritated to have to
cover for people who were already paid a damn sight more than they were.

There was always a chance that the boys might rescue a pretty girl from blazing house...

There is always a need to maintain a careful balance between readiness fc military operational tasks on the one hand and supporting the civilian communit in a MACA tasks on the other. Senior officers had warned that the plan to us the Armed Forces as replacement firefighters would prevent Britain fror supporting any American invasion of Iraq. With thousands of British soldier deployed on firefighting, the army's ability to undertake operations elsewher would be limited. One commanding officer told *The Telegraph*, "The vas majority of the soldiers committed to Op FRESCO will come from the army that's almost a third of its entire strength," he said. "It will in effect mean tha the army is grounded while the strike is on."

In the event, the soldiers did a great job and the firemen in due cours returned to duty.

The other of the four F's with which I was involved was Foot-and-Mout Disease (FMD). FMD is a severe, highly contagious viral disease which cause illness in cows, pigs, sheep, goats, deer. It spreads incredibly quickly and easily and so is exceedingly hard to control once it has broken out. In February 200 the first hint that foot-and-mouth had reached the UK came when an inspectio at an abattoir in Essex showed highly suspicious signs of the disease in 27 pigs

The outbreak of foot and mouth was headline news across the nation, and i quickly became apparent that the government had made the decision to ask th military for assistance. The foot and mouth quickly spread and within a matte of days had reached Scotland, with the first cases confirmed on 1 Marc following tests on two farms, both in Dumfries and Galloway. Just a few day later funeral pyres were lit on the two farms in Scotland to incinerate animal affected by the foot-and-mouth crisis.

The army was brought into Dumfries and Galloway to help with a pre emptive cull by providing logistical support and helping to organise the slaughte of animals across the region.

I had no thought that this might involve me until I was summoned to Arm Headquarters (HQ 2 Division) in Craigiehall, Edinburgh. I was tasked to go tc Dumfries and visit the troops who had already been deployed there. "Visit you own soldiers who are down there, have a look at how things are going, and drop in and see me on the way back home." It sounded innocent enough. I discovered at my own commanding officer had just been appointed to lead the military ontribution to what was happening in Dumfries and Galloway. It was early lays, but it did seem that the army was increasingly providing the infrastructure nd administration for a quickly developing operation.

The next day I fed back to the assistant chaplain general, my friend Rev John Whitton. Our discussion quickly confirmed that there was need for a chaplain to e based in Dumfries.

"So, are you free?" he asked. It was unheard of for a TA chaplain to be ppointed to care for regular army troops and oversee a regular chaplain.

"Well, yes, I suppose," I replied with even less confidence than my response mplied.

John was later to tell me that when the general officer commanding 2nd Division had instructed him to make sure that adequate spiritual and welfare over was being provided for the men and women being deployed to work on ne harrowing and emotionally draining foot-and-mouth MACA task, John had ooked at the various chaplains who might be available and decided that I was ne 'man for the job'. He prepared a list of all the Regular and all the TA haplains in Scotland at that time and went back upstairs to see the general.

John Whitton's suggestion, 'I think we should appoint Padre Stephen Blakey, sir,' was met with what would probably have been a pretty typical egular army response in those days. "No, no, we need a regular guy." John roduced his list of possible contenders with their operation experience, and the iOC backed down, and I got the job.

Christine and I were living in an old church manse in Abercrombie, North East Fife at the time. We had sheep in the fields adjacent to the house, and so we new straight away that once I moved down to Dumfries I wouldn't be just lriving home for a casual visit from time to time. The military provided a hire ehicle and I moved into a hotel for the duration of my appointment.

The epidemic in Scotland was very large: in addition to the confirmed cases vhich were found on 187 farms, 193 dangerous contacts were identified, and nother 188 in the contiguous 3km sheep and pig cull. In all, these culls iccounted for 735,5000 animals slaughtered in Scotland.

There was enormous emotional strain on everyone concerned. and it was listressing work for the soldiers. It was good for me as their Padre to be able to e there with them, but it was surely more distressing for the farmers and their

families and workers, who had to stand by and watch their precious livestoc
being killed.

Movement of vehicles and people throughout the area of the infection an
the contiguous cull was strictly restricted. Only those who had authority wer
allowed on to, or off from, the farms, and so I was often the only person fro
the caring professions with access to the farming community whose lives wer
being so severely and harshly devastated. There was little I could say, though
did seek to bring some comfort and support.

These were dark days, and the soldiers had a horrible job to do, but it wa
good to be able to support them in the midst of all the anguish.

* * * * *

There was another 'F' of course, Flight Pan Am 103.

Pan Am Flight 103 was the routine Pan Am flight from Frankfurt to Detroi
via London and New York. On 21 December 1988 at 19:03 hours, the aircra
operating the Transatlantic leg of the route, was destroyed by a bomb, killing al
243 passengers and 16 crew in what became known as the 'Lockerbie Bombing'
Large sections of the aircraft crashed onto residential areas of Lockerbie, killin
11 more people on the ground.

By 20:00 hours that evening 1 RHF was tasked to stand-to 200 all ranks t
provide military assistance. The advanced party left Edinburgh at 02:00 hours o
22 December with the main body following in two convoys. The Battalion ha
two chaplains at that time, as Padre John Shields was in the process of handin
over to Padre Michael Scouler. Both padres were in the second part of the mai
body.

In his report *Reflections of Padre 1RHF*, Rev John Shields tells of th
unbelievably harrowing task undertaken by 1 RHF who spent three day
collecting corpses from the countryside around Lockerbie.

He writes in his conclusion:

*I hope and pray that I never have to participate in anything like this again
but I think it was essential to have been present with my soldiers, firstl
because it was important for them, but secondly it was essential that
experienced something of the horror which they felt. In retrospect, the event
of these days before Christmas underline for me the importance of th*

chaplain's presence with his soldiers at times of stress. In a very stark way it reinforces that we are first and foremost ministers to soldiers – not families' officers. At Lockerbie the men found themselves confronted with situations beyond anything they had seen in their lives, and for many it triggered off quite deep spiritual thoughts.

I am absolutely convinced (and I think that the commanding officer would agree with me) that the presence of chaplains was a major asset.

Men and women sign up for military service for all sorts of different reasons. ew who serve a full career could have any idea of the variety of tasks that would ome their way in the service of Queen and Country and in the causes of peace nd justice. Whatever they end up doing, and wherever they serve, chaplains will e close by, providing whatever support is required.

Chapter 12

Serving on the Fence

"A nation that cannot control its borders is not a nation." — US Presiden Ronald Reagan

It is perhaps not surprising that I have spent much of my life accompanyin soldiers who have been deployed to observe, patrol, protect or enforce man-mad borders. Armies only exist because human beings struggle to live at peace wit one other. As individuals, families, religions and nations we are wonderfull adept at finding reasons for being upset with our neighbours. These areas of friction all to easily turn into threats and counter-threats with the border betwee us often being the only thing that stops us from physical conflict. And so th border becomes a hugely important dynamic in the maintenance of peace.

As a Christian minister I find myself held in a tension of, on the one hand firmly believing in the cause of peace, while on the other strongly convince that, as Jesus Christ himself commented, there will be wars and rumours of wa until the end of time. We must work and pray for peace, and for the defeat of th war-makers. 'Blessed are the peacemakers.' But we should never be naïve enough to think that humanity has within itself the resources or the skills to creat worldwide lasting peace. And so, borders will continue to exist, and the work o the military to make these borders effective will continue, and chaplains wil continue to find themselves in all sorts of unexpected locations supporting thei soldiers who are serving on a fence.

My first experience of a military border was in the Caribbean in the sprin of 1978 when I covered for Padre Matthew Robertson during his R&R (Rest an Recuperation) from Belize. Chaplains on operations normally have their R&F extended by a week or so to allow them some extra time to give additiona pastoral support to the families and Rear Party. (Rear Party is now more usuall nown as the ROG Rear Operations Group perhaps to defray the opinion that those not deployed on operations were left back at home having an easy life, enjoying a party while their comrades risked life and limb.)

In the first half of 1978 the British army operation in Belize was covered by the whole battalion of KOSB, who were based in Airport Camp in the North, and two companies of RHF who covered Toledo district in the South of the country including Punta Gorda and Rideau Camps. The name of the former British Crown Colony of British Honduras had been changed to Belize on 1 June 1973 in anticipation of complete independence but the negotiations between the UK and Guatemala were long and drawn out and even after final independence was agreed in 1981 some elements remained unresolved.

At the centre of the disagreement was Guatemala's understanding of the 859 Treaty between the UK and Guatemala. While Britain believed that the Treaty settled the borders of an area which was already under British dominion, Guatemala's view was that they would give up their territorial claim on British Honduras, only after a number of conditions were met. This included the construction of a road from Guatemala to the Caribbean coast. The UK never did build that road, and so in 1884 Guatemala said that it would repudiate the Treaty, though it never actually followed up on the threat. There was a continuing concern, however, that the military dominated regime of Guatemala might take matters into their own hands, and so British troops were deployed to keep an eye on the Belize-Guatemala border.

The southern border of Belize is defined by the Sarstoon River which flows into the Gulf of Honduras, part of the Caribbean Sea. The border with Guatemala follows the river upstream from the coast, for about 25 miles pretty much due west towards Modesto Mendez in Guatemala, where it abruptly turns 90 degrees almost due north and heads in a straight line for the Mexican border about 100 miles away.

The British army had an OP (Observation Post) on top of a cliff overlooking this corner of the border. It was the closest point at which a major Guatemalan road approached the southern part of Belize, and the cliff top provided a good view across into Guatemala and of any potential threat. The OP was manned by a section of eight men who, in between keeping an eagle eye on the enemy, seemed to spend most of their time sunbathing, using a coconut oil extract as protection from the sun. It did look rather as if the oil might in fact be frying rather than protecting the skin of these normally whiter than white jocks from the West Coast of Scotland. (If you have ever been in George Square, Glasgow on the occasional sunny day when many of the young men strip off their shirts you will know that there is a white which is even whiter than that produced by Persil. Other brands are available!)

I accompanied Company Commander, Major Colin Dunbar, on his weekly inspection of the OP, and broke international law by swimming across the Sarstoon River into Guatemala. I don't suppose the Guatemalans were very concerned and it encouraged my Jocks that their young Padre was as daft as they were.

That connection with the soldiers continued a week or so later when another group invited me to accompany them on a day out to the Cays. We didn't break any international laws that day, but we did end up being stranded overnight on a Caribbean island.

One of the great joys of serving overseas is the opportunity offered to experience the local culture, cuisine and countryside. All of this does have to be fitted in alongside military duties and responsibilities, and it usually works out well. The exceptions more often than not involve alcoholic beverage, and it has to be said that the RHF Jocks in Belize did seem to manage to consume sufficient local rum most evenings ('Green Stripe' and others) to make the morning fitness regime hard to bear.

On this particular day I was asked along on a trip to the Cays. Cays are small low islands situated on a coral reef platform, where the reef rises permanently above the sea level. Imagine a sandy beach, a couple of palm trees, a gentle warm breeze, a scattering of wild grasses, blue sky and the most enticing blue green Caribbean Sea. A local lad in his rusty old boat with a small outboard motor transported a dozen Jocks and me out to this island, which was about the size of four football pitches. The main piece of technology on board was a huge ghetto blaster that we soon learnt was so that our Caribbean friend could listen to the Sunday afternoon football commentary. More important to us was the supply of beer and sandwiches which the quartermaster had provided to help us through the day.

It was all truly idyllic. *This is the life*, I thought to myself as I stretched out on the white sand after a quick paddle in the Caribbean Sea. Join the army and travel the world. It was, of course, too good to last. A few of the jocks had managed to persuade the local guy to let them take his boat further offshore so at they could dive into deeper water. No harm in that I thought, reflecting that was the only officer in the party but confident that nothing could go wrong.

Well, nothing except for that warm, gentle off-shore breeze which was gently udging the boat further and further from shore, and the total lack of oars on the oat, the unwillingness of our local man to be a hero and help out (someone had 1st scored a goal on the radio and his understanding of English had suddenly eteriorated) and the fact that the guys on the boat hadn't the faintest idea how start the outboard motor. We tried shouting outboard motor starting 1structions from the shore, we attempted to swim out to help them only to iscover that by now the boat was drifting away faster than we could swim wards it, and then we struggled against the tide and the breeze to regain the hore and stood bedraggled watching as the boat, and its four occupants with no hade from the tropical sun, slowly disappeared towards the horizon, probably ot into the open Caribbean Sea but towards the Guatemalan coast and the nemy.

My head buzzed for a while. Surely, we couldn't just sit here and do nothing, ut that was in fact the only option available to us. The army knew where we had one and in due course, they would come looking for us and, in the meantime, e had sun and sand and beer and sandwiches. "What's not to like, Padre?" In act the only complaint I heard all night was, "Shame there aren't any women to hare the romance!"

We slept under the palm trees, had fresh coconut milk for breakfast and the rmy arrived in a couple of landing craft to take us home. A local Belizean ishing boat had rescued the men on the drifting boat, and all was well. Well, all vas well except for the jokes at the Padre's expense. From the feeding of the 5,000 to Jesus walking on the water, the Bible stories were reshaped and thrown ack at me. But, hi, if you can't take a joke the army is probably the wrong place or you. I even featured on the front page of the *Belize Bugle*, the families' 1ewsletter produced back in Edinburgh.

I think the only other time I might have illegally crossed an international border was on exercise in Italy with the Scots Guards. We were based in North East Italy for four weeks on Exercise PONTE VECCHIO. A company of UK troops exchanged locations with a company of Italian soldiers. I had persuaded the commanding officer to include me on the trip. It was another of these 'work hard, play hard' situations. We exercised on dried-up river beds on the foot slopes of the Italian Alps, used some wonderful field kitchen equipment which the Italian army had never unwrapped, and surprised our hosts by staying out on the training area overnight rather than returning to the comfort and security of the barracks.

The 'playing hard' included, so I was reminded recently at a Third Guards Club dinner, a challenge from some young Italian officers about who could drink the most of their national drink. Huge quantities of grappa and whisky were consumed. It has been suggested that my involvement added to our victory, but I couldn't possibly comment.

It was the same group of young Italian army officers who took us out for dinner one evening. We were a little surprised to discover that we ended up in a restaurant in Yugoslavia, having crossed the border via a small country road. It was a lovely dinner and we quietly passed back over the border under cover of darkness.

While it might be easy to blame the intransigence of the Guatemalans for the
eed to militarise the Belize – Guatemala border, it is much more of a challenge
to find a succinct explanation for the huge military presence on the Northern
eland – Republic of Ireland border in the 1980s. In 1972 at the height of the
roubles in Northern Ireland there were 27,000 British troops based in the
rovince. There seemed to be endless aspects to the problems behind the struggle
to create and maintain the rule of law in this part of the United Kingdom and, in
apport of the civilian police, the British army tried a wide range of measures to
mit the effectiveness of terrorist organisations and of those who sought to take
dvantage of the disruptions to make financial gain through cross border
muggling and other illegal activities.

In the mid-1980s the decision was made to build a series of watchtowers
long the border with the Irish Republic which would allow the army to observe
aore clearly the movements of people, animals and goods across the border, and
to gather more accurate intelligence.

Soon after the erection of these watchtowers I was mobilised with 1st
Battalion Scots Guards for a six-month tour based in Bessbrook Mill in South
Armagh. My one previous Op BANNER tour had been with 1 KOSB in West
Belfast in 1979. During that tour I lived in Flax Street Mill with a small team of
fficers as part of the Echelon. The officers consisted of Maj Ken Fraser the
Quartermaster, Capt George Wood the assistant adjutant, Capt Bill Coulthard the
aymaster, Capt Norman Arnott the Motor Transport officer and me. We had an
fficers' mess all to ourselves. In the midst of all the trouble and danger being
xperienced by the rest of the Battalion, it really did feel that we were being
reated like lords. We were well fed and watered and had comfortable living and
leeping accommodation.

The Battalion's TAOR (Territorial Area of Responsibility) was West Belfast
vith the Battalion HQ at Springfield Road Police Station. Our three company
ocations were Fort Monagh, North Howard Street and Whiterock. It was a
langerous place for our soldiers and there were a number of serious incidents
luring our four months there, but in the midst of all the tension and stress there
vas room for pleasure and enjoyment.

As padre, I had my own civilian vehicle, a mustard-coloured Ford Escort
vhich was one of quite a number of such vehicles owned by the military. I also
1ad a pretty large clerical collar which I ensured was clearly visible at all times.
Quartermaster Ken Fraser was on his final tour of duty with the Battalion prior

153

to heading off to Brunei for a two-year posting with the Sultan's forces. Ke would sometime use me as his private chauffeur. "Padre, I need to go out o private business, and I would like you to accompany me!" i.e., drive him he and there. Ken would sign out a Walther PK380 pistol which he would stic down the back of his trousers and off we would go, sometimes shopping ar sometimes socialising. Ken's late wife was from Northern Ireland and he seeme to have endless connections and therefore received many invitations. I, of cours was dressed like a clergyman throughout all of this and so the opportunities f misbehaving were extremely limited.

During my four months in West Belfast we held Sunday worship each wee in each of our five locations. In those days each Scottish Infantry unit had i own military band (brass and woodwind) as well as its Pipes and Drums. Th Regimental military Band was made up of professional musicians who had secondary role as stretcher bearers during armed conflict. The P's and D's wei professional soldiers with a role as the machine gun platoon but spent much o their time piping and drumming. This ready supply of music was a godsend t the chaplain.

The Regimental Band came with us on that tour of duty in West Belfast, wit a few musicians in each of our locations. Every Sunday I would visit all fiv locations and the Bandmaster, Mr Butler, would come with me. He would b supported by a couple of lads from that particular location and they would lea the singing for our church service. This helped the Bandmaster to see his me and saved the troops from having me lead their singing unaccompanied. Thes services were important opportunities not just for their spiritual benefit, but als because they brought everyone based at that location together for 20 minute once a week, providing a break in a routine which was pretty much the same da in and day out seven days a week, and because they marked the completion o another week in our seventeen-week tour of duty.

I am not a very talented musician, but I do read music and at various time of my life have played the trombone and the guitar, though neither very well. I Berlin, with the Black Watch, I would from time to time drop into the Regimenta Band practice room and try my best to play along with the trombone section o the military band. The guys were always very polite to me.

I still use the guitar quite often to lead worship in my church, but I think th only time I played the trombone to lead worship was at a church muster i Rhuleben Fighting City in Berlin. The Black Watch have a strong tradition o hurch services of which they are very proud, and perhaps more than other scottish units were always keen for the padre to hold church services on the raining area during exercises. Rhuleben Fighting City was a FIBUA training facility. FIBUA stands for Fighting in Built Up Areas. Soldiers have been known to call it FISH training – 'fighting in somebody's hoose'. The video of me reading worship is still available on YouTube 'In the Highest Tradition', episode ix.

My second Op BANNER Tour, with the Scots Guards in 1985, was in total contrast. I did still have a car, but it was only for driving north from Bessbrook, mainly for visits to the brigade headquarters in Lisburn and to the military wing of Musgrave Park Hospital in Belfast. Almost all other travel was by helicopter. Bessbrook Mill was reckoned at that time to be the busiest heliport in Europe.

We had company locations at Crossmaglen and Forkhill, close to the Irish Border, from which the solders would patrol out on foot but which I could only get to by helicopter. In addition to the main company bases we also manned the newly constructed watchtowers which had only just been built along the border with the Republic of Ireland. These were equipped with some very high-tech surveillance equipment and, of course, hated by the civilian population.

Each tower was about twenty feet high and topped with a bullet proof observation pod, large enough to hold two or three soldiers on duty. This observation post, with 360 degree all round vision, was positioned high up on top of a scaffolding type structure, which stood over the top of an underground bunker which provided living, cooking and sleeping accommodation. A team of eight to ten soldiers would man each tower for a week at a time. The only safe access was by helicopter, and all the supplies and visitors came that way. Each watchtower had a Heli landing site in an adjacent field.

So, the only way I could visit my men, when they were on duty in a tower, was to hitch a lift on a helicopter flight. I developed a routine of booking my flights the previous evening and then reporting to the airhead at the arranged flight time, often to find that there was an important military priority and that I had been bumped off the flight and would have to wait until another slot appeared. The flight programme was run by the Buzzard Team, our own specially trained planners and air traffic controllers.

"Right, Padre, there's a seat on this one!" and I would join the group of men rushing out to board the helicopter. Most nights I would get back to my own bed in Bessbrook Mill, but it was never guaranteed and, as the helicopter dropped me

off in the muddy field next to a watchtower, I could never be quite sure how lon
I would be there for.

You might well ask if it would not have made more sense for me just to wa
and see the soldiers when they got back from their week on duty in the towe
and on some cold, wet, windy days I might have found my thoughts drifting tha
way as well. chaplains have always found that being alongside the soldiers in th
midst of the discomfort and the challenges of their work goes a long way t
opening to door to chat and conversation. We are part of the team, and take th
rough with the smooth, just like everybody else.

Driving around Northern Ireland brought its own challenges. We wer
strongly encouraged to vary our routes, and certainly to take a different roa
home to the one taken on the way out. This would often result in me wanderin
off the main Belfast to Newry road to follow a winding country lane back towar
Bessbrook. This worked well on sunny days when I knew that if I just kep
heading south, vaguely towards the sun, then I would in due course hit the Newr
– Armagh road with signposts to Bessbrook. The sun however was neve
guaranteed in Northern Ireland.

* * * * *

The international border which dominated British army activity throughou
most of my time as a regular chaplain was, of course, the Inner German Borde
which divided West and East Germany, known formally as Federal Republic o
Germany and the Democratic German Republic. At the end of the Second Worl
War Germany had been divided into British, French, American and Russiar
Sectors. In time the British, French and American Sectors became Wes
Germany, and the Russian sector became Communist East Germany. The Inne
German Border divided these two nations. While we in the West would no doub
have preferred to treat this as a normal international border, it was in fact wher
the NATO and the Warsaw Pact collided, and so it held a very special status.

The place where I did get up close to East Germany was in Berlin. I was
posted to Berlin as chaplain to 1st Battalion the Black Watch 1987 after a five-
year attachment with the Scots Guards. News of my posting came through a
shrouded message from the then DCG. Prior to heading off on our Op BANNER
tour in South Armagh I phoned MOD chaplains to ask if they could tell me what
was likely to happen to me when I returned from Northern Ireland. My time with

st Battalion Scots Guards had been extended so that I could go with them on the ix-month tour, meaning that I would complete a full five years with them, so I as well overdue a posting to another unit and location. We were about to send ur daughter Barbara off to boarding school in Edinburgh, but we would have elayed this if our next posting was somewhere in Scotland.

"DCG, I wonder if you know yet where I will be posted to when I return rom South Armagh?" I asked.

"Well," came the reply, "I do know what we have planned, but it is too early) confirm anything." So I explained why I was keen to know, and actually why ie whole family was keen to know.

"All I can say Stephen is that you are down to be posted to Germany, quite ar east in Germany, to a Scottish unit, and one of your former units will be based n the same city."

I could never say that the Deputy Chaplain General had just informed me hat I was to be posted to The Black Watch who were due to do a two-year tour n Berlin, and that the KOSB were also in Berlin at that time, but that is what iappened, I went off on Op BANNER with 1SG, Barbara went off to prep school n Edinburgh, and Christine began to plan for another move overseas.

Our first journey to Berlin was by air when we flew into RAF Gatow. The vhole family was together, and we were collected off the RAF flight by the 'amilies Office staff of 1 BW. That night we lay in bed and listened to the firing n a nearby rifle range. Next day I asked who was on the ranges last night, to be old that it was the Russians conducting rifle practice on the local East German anges. The enemy were not far away. In fact, they were so close that the fence vhich separated East Germany from West Berlin actually ran through the lower)art of our barracks in Kladow.

The mention of West Berlin for many people will go hand in hand with the iame Checkpoint Charlie. It is easy to forget that there was also a Checkpoint Alpha and a Checkpoint Bravo. The ABC of checkpoints. Alpha was the crossing)ver the Inner German Border between West Germany and East Germany, Bravo vas the crossing from East Germany into West Berlin. Charlie was the crossing from West Berlin into East Berlin. Checkpoint Alpha and Checkpoint Bravo vere joined by a 110-mile-long concrete motorway. Allied personnel required ipecial passes to travel this road, they had to stay strictly within the 110 km/hr ipeed limit and were not allowed to leave the route. As well as all the controls :xercised by the West German and East German police at the appropriate locations, movement of British military and their dependants was all ve[r]y carefully monitored and controlled by the Royal military Police. Arriving ear[ly] at the next checkpoint would indicate speeding and result in a warning or wors[e].

Serving in Berlin was a very special experience. We were there as powers [of] occupation and so enjoyed a number of special privileges. One of these was [a] Putzfrau (cleaning lady or 'daily') provided on the Berlin budget. The numb[er] of hours she worked was determined by your rank. There was also the FR[IS] (Family Ration Issue System) which was a response to the Berlin Blockade (2[4] June 1948 – 12 May 1949), one of the first major international crises of the Co[ld] War. The Soviet Union blocked the Western Allies' railway, road, and can[al] access to the sectors of Berlin under Western control. The Soviets then demande[d] that the Western Allies withdrew the newly introduced Deutsche Mark fro[m] West Berlin, stating that they would only drop the blockade when this w[as] achieved.

To overcome the increasing shortage of supplies for the city's population [of] 2 million, the Western Allies organised the Berlin airlift (26 June 1948 – 3[0] September 1949) to carry supplies to the people of West Berlin.

After it was all over, and to reduce the impact of a repeat of the blockad[e], the British military stockpiled a range of foodstuff. In order to ensure that th[e] various items did not go past their 'best before' date, and to turn the stock ove[r,] these were offered to military families through the FRIS system. Each househol[d] was issued with a book of A3 sized forms which listed the wide range [of] foodstuffs which was available at a reduced cost. You completed your order f[or] the coming week and left it on your doorstep in a metal FRIS bin. Later in th[e] day your order was picked up, and the goods you had ordered last week wer[e] dropped off.

A fairly broad range of items was listed, or so it seemed to start with. Afte[r] a few months, however, the range started to feel somewhat limited. We a[ll] become experts at cooking the lovely legs of lamb, and the smell of freshl[y] toasted teacake will still bring back memories for many Berlin veterans.

West Berlin sat like an island in the middle of a hostile Communist sea. [It] was surrounded on three sides by a fence between it and East Germany, and b[y] the Berlin Wall which stood across the middle of the city between West and Eas[t] Berlin on the fourth side. We had no role in policing the fence or the Wall, an[d] really there was little need. The Communist forces were very focussed o[n] opping any of their people escaping into the capitalist West Berlin. We lived ith these strictures as just part of everyday life.

* * * * *

In 1984 we flew out to Hong Kong to join 1st Battalion Scots Guards and I nce again found myself on an international order. Along with the other military nits in the province we took our turn serving on the fence between Communist ainland China and the British colony of Hong Kong.

Hong Kong stirs the romantic imagination of many people, but its past is eeply grounded in a less than honourable chapter of British history. The use of e opium market to fund our international trade, and the resultant human misery, as certainly not our Empire's finest hour.

The UK took ownership of Hong Kong Island in 1842 through the Treaty of Janking. The land governed by the British grew to include the Kowloon eninsula and then in 1898 it was extended to include the New Territories on a 9-year lease, which would run out, and did run out, in 1997. The inclusion of e rural New Territories provided much-needed water and space which had llowed the colony to prosper.

There had been free movement between Hong Kong and mainland China ntil 1949, when the People's Republic of China was established. Hong Kong hen experienced a huge influx of refugees from Communist China, and this opulation boom led to severe shortages in housing and social services in the erritory.

Over the next 30 years or so the Hong Kong government tried various olicies to allow a level of controlled movement of people from mainland China nto Hong Kong but these failed to halt the influx of immigrants and were bolished in 1980.

When we arrived in 1984, the situation was that all illegal immigrants were epatriated to China immediately. All Hong Kong residents had to carry their dentity cards in public areas. A one-way permit had been introduced by the 'eople's Republic of China setting a limit of 150 residents from mainland China er day to leave the mainland permanently in order to settle in Hong Kong.)espite this high number there were still many others who were desperate to get nto Hong Kong.

Most nights individuals, and sometimes whole families, would be caug
trying to escape into Hong Kong from the Republic of China. British troo
would chase them down in the undergrowth and hand them over to the Roy
Hong Kong Police. At 12 noon the next day the Hong Kong Immigratic
Officials would hand over the previous night's 'catch' of illegal immigrants
the Lo Wo Border Crossing Point.

In many ways this was pretty routine soldiering for our troops. They didn
like the idea that these Chinese Illegal Immigrants (known as 'IIs') who ha
rightly or wrongly been courageous enough to run the gauntlet of th
international border were now being passed back over to the Communi
government that they were trying to escape from. There was no doubt that th
fate they were returning to would be worse than the one they had just tried t
escape from. Having said that, our soldiers had a job to do though much of th
job required a lot of hanging around.

It was in the midst of some of the 'hanging around' that two of our soldie
decided to liven their lives up a little. We were operating the well-accepte
British army 'two can rule' whereby troops at a certain low level of readines
were allowed two cans of beer per day. This was all carefully monitored, an
those above certain level of responsibility were excluded. For many soldiers 'tw
cans' was a waste of time. Jocks especially would reckon that two cans just mad
you thirsty for a 'proper drink', and so not worth bothering with.

On this particular evening, which was to result in The South China Mornin
Post headline, with white lettering on a black banner 'The Night Two Scot
Guards Went on the Rampage', one of our company chefs, who had finished hi
duty for the day and had nothing to do until getting up in time to cook breakfa
the next morning, managed to persuade whoever was issuing the beer that he wa
signing on behalf of six men, and left the store with 12 cans of lager.

After he and his mate had downed the lot, they really did feel ready for
party. But where? The obvious location was the Wanchai area in downtow
Hong Kong Island, 20 miles away. The Wanchai was a favourite location for
good night out for the lads. To get there the chef and his chum decided to 'ho
wire' an army Land Rover, and for good measure thought that it would useful t
be armed. They managed to convince one of the younger soldiers that his weapo
was required for checking by the armourer and, not knowing any better, h
handed it over.

160

Boozed up, armed and mobile, they set off south. The possibilities for disaster were endless. Most weeks there were reports in the local press about the Hong Kong police shooting criminals, and this escapade was surely heading in that direction. They had a drink in the Wanchai, headed off to North Point to see if any of the battalion wives (whose men were up on the border on duty) fancied a little romance, and then, having failed at that, they decided that flying home to UK would be a better idea. It was a series of events which if you made it all up people would laugh you out of town.

After six hours of madness which included a couple of vehicle hijackings, a number of shots being fired, three hostages taken and Kai Tak airport being closed down, the two began to sober up, handed over their weapons and surrendered.

The next day I sat in the back of the CO's staff car with my fairly new commanding officer Lt Col Kim Ross as we drove back up to the Border and I wondered, *What does the chaplain say to offer support in such a situation?* Having stammered my way through some fairly meaningless 'what a difficult thing to happen at the beginning of your time in command, sir', Kim just laughed.

"No one was hurt! The guardsmen will always find some mischief to get up to! It could have been so much worse."

It was worse, of course, for the two soldiers themselves, who spent some time in Hong Kong prison before being sent back to complete their sentences in the UK. One of them was married, and it did take time for his wife to understand the seriousness of the night's events. When Sid Carnegie, the Families' Officer, visited her to explain that her husband was under arrest and wouldn't be home for a while, her initial question was, "Will the fine come off this month's pay or next?"

Time has moved on, and that particular Border and the situation in Hong Kong, while still of great interest to us, is no longer under British control. There are, and will continue to be, borders and fences and boundaries for our military to police, though not all of the fences needing to be patrolled are outside Great Britain.

After returning to UK from Hong Kong in 1984 I spent two consecutive Easter holiday weekends on yet another fence with solders of the Scots Guards. They were supporting the civilian police patrolling the fence at Greenham Common. Greenham Common Women's Peace Camp was established in September 1981 to protest against nuclear Cruise weapons being sited at RAF

Greenham Common in Berkshire, England. When protestor numbers increase the military was often called in to assist, and the padre turned up to raise morale. At the height of the protest 30,000 women held hands around the six-mil perimeter of the base.

This fence within our own country was easily identified, but many of th political and historical dynamics which divide, and separate societies are les visible, as I was to learn during my final operational tour in 2005.

Chapter 13
Balkans 2005

"Bosnia is under my skin. It's the place you cannot leave behind. I was obsessed by the nightmare of it all; there was this sense of guilt, and an anger that has become something much deeper over these last years." — Paddy Ashdown, High Representative for Bosnia and Herzegovina 2002–2006

Late in 2004, Christine and I were living in the town of Ayr on the west coast of Scotland. I was on a break from parish ministry, working as a life coach and running a Life Coach Training organisation. For some time I had been fascinated by the fact that a surprising number of goal setting, and life-coaching concepts and programmes were remarkably similar to the teaching of the Bible. I really enjoyed reading books on this subject and felt sure that I would actually be quite good at using these techniques to assist other people to improve their lives. I was going through some difficulties in my personal life which made me question if I was righteous enough to serve God, and escaping from parish ministry had seemed a good idea... but how could I do this? An article in an American Christian magazine suggested that well over 50% of clergy were unfulfilled in their work and would change profession if they just knew how to. I suspected that the statistics would not be all that different in the UK. Perhaps becoming a life coach would provide a way to take a break. So, I started to explore the possibilities and soon realised that there was, at that time, no professional body or accreditation for life coaches.

The owner of Life Coach UK was very encouraging. "Just go ahead. Set up Life Coach Scotland. Get in there before anybody else steals the name. If you are any good, then you will succeed. If you are useless, you will learn soon enough." So I threw myself into it, scrounged as much training material as I could find, learnt as much as possible, registered the business and the website, and in a reasonably short period of time I appointed myself as the Director of Life Coach Scotland and Life Coach Scotland Training School, and soon after became the Scottish Director of the Association for Coaching, and was appointed the Director of Ethics for the European Coaching Institute.

I really enjoyed the work which ranged from assisting the Glasgow Mentoring Network to provide and oversee mentors for unemployed young people in Glasgow through the UK Government's New Deal programme, to coaching my own personal clients, while also running a training programme for potential Life Coaches in the skills they would require to create their own Life Coaching practice. I rewrote our training material and used it provide in-service training (INSET) for schoolteachers, providing another income stream.

Part of the joy, for me, of being a Life Coach with paying clients was that the individuals all really did want to achieve new things in their life, and so they were willing to invest time and finances in the process and were focussed and disciplined in working with me. So often in church we seem to work with folk who have very little desire to change, sometimes just wanting the clergy to massage their morale and confirm them in their long-held beliefs.

I soon found that I was a pretty good life coach and had most of the gifts and talents required to be a moderate success. My main shortcoming was financial planning and management, and this sadly meant that the whole project was built on somewhat shaky business foundations. I wasn't sure where it was all going. I loved the work and while it all looked pretty successful the future did feel uncertain, and then the phone rang…

Throughout my five years away from the parish I had continued to serve as a TA chaplain, as padre to 52nd Lowland Regiment. Having friends in the right places meant that I picked up quite a lot of extra military work. As they say, 'It's not what you know, it's who you know, that counts.' When Rev John Whitton was assistant chaplain general of the British army 2nd Division Headquarters based at Craigiehall just outside Edinburgh, he appointed me as the senior chaplain of the troops mobilised during the Foot and Mouth outbreak in 2001 and Dr Iain Barclay, who throughout this period was staff chaplain at Craigiehall had arranged for me to provide cover for all sorts of vacancies. For example, I spent four weeks in Reindahlen in Germany providing pastoral cover while all the Regular chaplains based there enjoyed their summer leave. I went to the USA on TA summer camp with the Geordie Gunners (25 Field Regiment, Royal Artillery). I also covered quite a number of Army Cadet Force Summer Camps, d I became an itinerant teacher of ITD11 (Individual Training Directive o.11), the then moral standards teaching programme for the British army.

I was possibly the busiest non-regular army chaplain over these years, but mes had started to change and TA chaplains were beginning to be called up to over operational tasks alongside the regulars. Rev Jim Gibson and Rev Angus err were two of the first Church of Scotland Parish Ministers to be deployed to an operational theatre as TA chaplains, both of them serving in the Balkans the late 1990s.

It was against this background of my life coaching business feeling very nancially insecure, my on-going involvement with military chaplaincy, and the ew pattern of TA chaplains going on operations along with the hundreds of TA oldiers who were being mobilised, that I received a call from Rev John Whitton, ho by this time was deputy chaplain general at MOD Chaplains (Army).

John never called me on the phone, or perhaps I should say that he never alled unless he was after something. We were good friends but not good at eeping in touch. I was sitting on the train from Ayr to Glasgow, en route to an ppointment with a life coaching client, so I was in business mode, bright eyed nd bushy tailed.

It took John about three sentences to get to the point. "How do you fancy a ip to visit your old haunts in the Gulf?" he asked. I was not expecting this, and ll sorts of questions flooded my mind. Business, family, finances, fatalities.

"I don't know, John, I need to think about that. I'll get back to you."

"You've got two days and then I need a decision!" and he hung up.

That evening Christine and I talked long and hard. I really had no desire return to the Gulf. It just didn't feel right, but how could I say 'no' when so man of my TA soldiers were themselves being deployed, and not just deployed. I ha already conducted the funeral services for two 52nd Lowland soldiers who ha died in Iraq. Previously soldiers had signed up for the Territorials with no re expectation of actually going to war. We worked hard and played hard, at week drill nights, monthly training weekends and annual Summer Camp, but very fe did much more than that until it all began to change with the follow-up to t invasion of Iraq in 2004. Then TA soldiers were called up to work alongside t regular army, filling gaps in the manning structure. It was all very new and ve challenging. As a TA chaplain I supported those being deployed and the famili they left behind. I wasn't sure in myself if I could refuse to deploy as requeste and still hold my head up around my men, and of course six months on a milita salary would greatly please my bank manager.

Two days later I phoned MOD chaplains and asked to be put through to th deputy chaplain general. "DCG, I am really not at all keen to serve in the Gu but would be willing to give you six months to cover somewhere else. Perha this would free up another chaplain to fill the slot in the Gulf."

I don't remember if he bit my hand off there and then, but the offer wa certainly warmly received and immediately confirmed. As I was at that time sel employed, I had no civilian employment hoops to jump through and the proces for my mobilisation began straight away. I had imagined that John would arrang for me to cover a chaplain's post in the UK, or in a German garrison, but h appointed me to fill the post of the UK Senior chaplain in the Balkans, and I di so from March to November 2005.

After Jim Gibson and Angus Kerr had completed their deployment in Ira questions began to be asked within the Church of Scotland about the guideline for parish ministers who were TA chaplains being called up to serve alongsid the Regulars. How were they to be paid? What would happen to their stipends Who would look after their parish while they were serving the military? Wha would happen to their church pension rights? I have to say that most of us on th ground weren't too concerned about such details, but it was right that thes matters were properly dealt with. Rev Dr Iain Torrance was Convenor of th

Church of Scotland Chaplains Committee at the time, and his razor-sharp mind ensured that watertight regulations were put in place.

I wasn't working as a parish minister at the time so none of this applied to me, but my self-employed status did produce a number of other complications. I had to put Life Coach Scotland and Life Coach Scotland Training School into suspended animation and arrange for the MOD to cover my office rental costs during my deployment. I also had to begin thinking about how I would restart my income flow when the time came for me to return from the Balkans. Some of my clients and students were less than amused that I was leaving the country, but I did manage to find colleagues who would be able to provide a service for them which was possibly even better than what I was already delivering. As to the future, I decided that returning to parish ministry was probably the safest route and, through some quite remarkable turn of events, I managed to ensure that the vacant congregation of Glasgow, Shawlands was willing to wait until my return to welcome me as their new minister.

The process for TA personnel being deployed on operations had by this time become quite smooth and I had a fair knowledge of how it all worked having been part of the briefing team, preparing and supporting our own soldiers from 52 Lowland Regiment. The Reserves Training and Mobilisation Centre (RTMC) in Chilwell, had been developed to process members of the Territorial Army being mobilised on service overseas.

It always seemed a bit strange to me that personnel were taken all the way down to Chilwell before they had passed the required medical, dental and fitness tests for operational deployment. Those who failed were then sent back home. This was really awkward, especially as most of the Reservists had been through the process of informing their civilian employers that they had been mobilised, and the employers then having to adapt their business to take account of losing one of their team for six months or more. It was even more stressful for the families. One day their loved ones were preparing to head off for six months in some dangerous location, and the next they arrived back home having failed the mobilisation process. I was glad to be able to avoid all of this.

I headed off to Chilwell, attended all the various elements of the training and testing that applied to a chaplain going to the Balkans, and was allowed to go back home for a few days before flying off to Banja Luka in Bosnia and Herzegovina, home to the HQ UK NSE (National Support Element) of the international force EUFOR (European Force) which was engaged on

Operation ALTHEA overseeing the military implementation of the Dayton Agreement. My posting was as senior chaplain UK NSE Bosnia. EUFOR had nearly 7,000 troops from 33 member nations of which 22 were EU Member States and 11 were non-EU Troop Contributing Nations. The actual numbers and their nations when I took over are listed in Appendix G.

The Balkans have a chequered and confusing history and explaining the existence of British troops being based there in 2005 is not straightforward. The potted history at Appendix H goes some way to clarifying the situation.

The British contingent in Bosnia Herzegovina (BiH) numbered 727 and was mainly made up of 1st Battalion Argyll and Sutherland Highlanders. I was 'senior' chaplain because the Battalion had their own chaplain, Padre Rupert Jarvis. During my time there Rupert went back to UK on R&R for two weeks and I covered for him while he was away, becoming the temporary chaplain of 1 A and SH. These two weeks completed my collection of Scottish Infantry units giving me the unique privilege of having served at some stage with every element of the Scottish Infantry Battalions which would form the Royal Regiment of Scotland in 2006. I had served with the Royal Scots, the Royal Highland Fusiliers, the King's Own Scottish Borderers and the Black Watch as a regular chaplain, and then as a Reservist I had covered the Highlanders (Gordon Highlanders and the Queen's Own Highlanders) as senior chaplain Foot and Mouth, and now the Argyll and Sutherland Highlanders as the senior chaplain in the Balkans.

The Royal Regiment of Scotland was formed on 28 March 2008 from the old Scottish Infantry Regiments of the line. These regiments were amongst the oldest and boldest British fighting regiments, having fought in every corner of the world over the previous 400 years. The regular units which united that day were: The Royal Scottish Borderers, The Royal Highland Fusiliers, The Black Watch, The Highlanders and The Argyll and Sutherland Highlanders. These five Battalions, along with the two territorial Battalions 52nd Lowland and 51st Highland were presented with their first set of Royal Regiment of Scotland Colours by HM The Queen at a marvellous parade in Holyrood Park on 2 July 2011.

* * * * *

I arrived in the Metal Factory in Banja Luka on 22 March 2005 and took up my appointment as Senior chaplain. Despite all the briefings I had sat through ack in the UK it was still all very new and challenging. I had heard of the Metal actory in Banja Luka, but really had very little idea what to expect, and found ayself confronted with many surprises during my first few days.

On my first morning I reported to the Commander of UK NSE who was ased in Banja Luka. He informed me that the Commander of EUFOR wanted) see me as soon as possible. The Commander EUFOR was Major General)avid Leakey, who from 2010 to 2018 would hold the position of Gentleman Jsher of the Black Rod in the Palace of Westminster, our Houses of Parliament. n 2005, he was the first commander of EUFOR. His headquarters was in arajevo, so I booked a place on a helicopter and reported as requested.

It had been mentioned to me that General Leakey was looking to formalise n arrangement by which the Senior UK chaplain would become the senior haplain EUFOR, but my predecessor had decided to side step the suggestion intil I took up post, and I was pretty much left to come to my own decision. It eemed to me that if Rupert Jarvis was looking after the Argyll's then I was left vith about a couple of hundred other Brits spread round BiH and Kosovo and vith a sprinkling in Croatia and Montenegro. There wasn't even a proper UK haplain's office in Butmir Camp, Sarajevo as the previous one had been ubsumed into the soldiers' social club to make more room for the pool table.

The opportunity to become Senior chaplain of a 33-nation force, to work for ZUFOR, NATO, KFOR (Kosovo Force) and the UN, across the whole Balkan egion sounded as if it would be satisfying and exciting, so I accepted the general's appointment and spent the following seven months fulfilling this inique challenge. A new fully equipped and furnished office came with the job. When I expressed my admiration for the efficiency with which 'the system' had aroduced this spanking new senior chaplain's office, the general just smiled and said, "Well, I did suggest it would be a good idea!"

I very quickly ended up with three bed spaces (Banja Luka Metal Factory, Butmir Camp in Sarajevo, and the British Camp in Pristina in Kosovo) with three mobile phones, and access to a wide range of transportation including travel by oad with a driver in Banja Luka, my own vehicle in Sarajevo, helicopter flights aetween Banja Luka and Sarajevo, RAF Hercules flights down to Kosovo, and he occasional Greek military flights between Sarajevo and Kosovo.

Much time was spent hanging around airheads waiting for flights, and it was during these many hours that I became great friends with Squadron Leader Adrian Aderyn. Well, actually it is probably truer to say that we did spend a lot of time hanging around waiting for flights and that we became great friends i the officers' mess bar afterwards.

The Greek air trooping flights were the best of all. One day I reported t Sarajevo International Airport to check in for the trooper to Kosovo which wa then heading on to Athens. The Greeks had fewer than 200 soldiers serving i the Balkans but getting these guys home on leave was a high priority. Th security was all much less than anything the RAF required. I had just sat dow in the departure lounge when the announcement came across, "Good mornin; everyone, we are all here so we will just get going." It was at least 30 minute before we had expected to board. We scrambled onto the Hercules transpo plane, and it headed off. When we landed at Pristina, where about half a doze of us were disembarking, the plane came to a halt, the tail gate was lowered, an we were ushered off with the propellers still rotating. By the time we had walke to the safety of the terminal building the Greek aircraft was already in the air e route for home. Oh, that all air movement was so stress free!

The main RAF flight was a Hercules which left Brize Norton on Saturda mornings and refuelled at Hanover on its way to Banja Luka, where it woul drop off and pick up passengers before flying on to Pristina, Kosovo. Afte unloading everyone in Pristina the crew would then fly over to Bari in Italy fc an overnight stop, prior to a mirror image return flight 24 hours later. The 2· hours allowed duty personal from BiH sufficient time to deal with their busines in Kosovo, and then were able to get back 'home' to Banja Luka without havin; to hang around extra days waiting for return flights.

The RAF crew's overnight Bari stopover was explained to me as bein; essential 'for security reasons and for technical support resources' and havin; nothing to do with ensuring the comfort of the RAF personnel. I only discovere that this happened when one of my flights was disturbed by a mechanical fault.

Half a dozen of us were hanging around the terminal at Banja Luka when th routine trooper flight landed. There was some concern about the condition of on of the engines which seemed to be leaking a little fluid, but the problem wasn' sufficient to stop us taking off and heading south towards Kosovo.

Halfway through the flight the loadmaster came on to the intercom to inforn us that the pilot was worried that the engine might be more damaged than the had at first thought. He was concerned that while we would be able to land safel at Pristina, he was not convinced that we would manage to take off again. A:

eir technical support was actually in Bari, and as there was a lack of overnight ilitary security in Kosovo, he had decided that we would all fly directly to Italy.

Well, this was a turn up for the books, and to my mind was certainly more citing that my routine trip to KFOR. I had never been to Bari and the idea of 1 overnight stopover seemed very attractive. One of the best aspects of this dventure for us passengers was that we had nothing to organise. This was an AF responsibility, and the man with the credit card took over. We were all poked into a very nice hotel, fed and watered, and told that we should report to e reception at 09:00 hours on Sunday morning to be informed what was going happen next.

Well, what was going to happen next was that Adrian Aderyn and myself, ccompanied by Major Murdoch Macleod and his bagpipes, were heading owntown for a quiet drink. There is of course no such thing as a 'quiet drink' ith three Scotsmen and a set of pipes. The local Italians loved the pipe music, id we loved the local beer, and it was a great party. We had a wonderful evening id in the wee small hours weaved our way back to the hotel. Our arrival in drian's room for a night cap was spoilt first of all by the discovery that a revious hotel guest had drunk the beer in the mini bar and replaced it with water fore forcing the tops back on the bottles. More importantly was the sad news n the TV that Pope John Paul II had just passed away.

Sunday morning arrived and we wandered around Bari until it was time for our RAF friends to take us to Pristina and then almost immediately back to Banja Luka. I think the only person dissatisfied by the outing was the Chief of Staff UK NSE who was frustrated that he didn't manage to attend his monthly meeting with KFOR staff, and even more frustrated that he had made the fatal schoolboy error of not packing some 'civvies' in the bottom of his backpack, and so could not join the party downtown, and instead had spent the entire evening watching Italian TV in his hotel room.

Having a spare set of 'civvies' is a basic requirement anywhere in the world. There are of course other important items to pack when travelling, like a dress for the Royal Marines (who it is rumoured enjoy dressing up in women's clothing from time to time), but a set of civilian clothing is high up on the list. My two German chaplaincy colleagues who were based in Sarajevo with the large national contingent told me that none of them had civilian clothes with them. When they were mobilised on operations, they wore uniform all the time. Sadly this meant that they had to miss out on a couple of very enjoyable evenings which I organised for my international chaplaincy team at the Sarajevska Pivara ('brewery') in Sarajevo.

The Sarajevo Brewery was founded on 24 May 1864, and historians consider it the oldest industrial plant in Bosnia and Herzegovina. It is the only European brewery whose production was uninterrupted during the Ottoman Empire and the Austro-Hungarian Monarchy. In 1907, the Sarajevo Brewery became the largest brewery in the Austro-Hungarian Empire. Even in the most difficult period, during the Balkans conflict from 1992 to 1995, the Sarajevo Brewery did not cease production. Much more importantly it became a supply point for clean fresh drinking water for the residents of Sarajevo during the siege.

We all have our favourite cities. People will tell you of their love of Paris or Rome or Venice. I guess, prior to my tour of duty in the Balkans, I would have said that my favourite was Venice. I had been there a couple of times. My first visit was as padre to a company of Scots Guardsmen on Exercise PONTE VECCHIO in 1985. We were based in Cividale del Friuli in Northern Italy (called 'Civvy-dale' by the guardsmen!) for a four-week exchange exercise and were given a weekend trip to Venice for our R&R.

I thought Venice was the most romantic place in the world, despite the fact that I was accompanied by 100 troops from 1 Scots Guards. I vowed that I would return with my wife Christine, and we did so a few years later. That first trip involved me sharing a hotel room with three young single men. We had had a wonderful sunny day as tourists in the city, and I was enjoying a meal with three young officers before catching the bus back to the Cividale. Each of us had the option of staying in Venice overnight, or heading back to the barracks, and to return to Venice on the Sunday morning.

"Right gents, I'm off to catch the bus. See you tomorrow," I declared as the meal came to an end.

"Padre, why not just stay?"

I had presumed that they might not want the chaplain around all evening. "No, I don't want to cramp your style. And I haven't booked a hotel room."

After an offer of a place in their room, and a promise that all they were planning was to enjoy some more 'vino rosso', I decided to accept. I did stay, but it was a pretty uncomfortable night. There were three single beds, and these were of course all taken. My mattress was the marble floor, my pillow was my jacket, and my duvet was a towel.

In the morning, after a pretty sleepless night, when they all headed down to the hotel restaurant for breakfast, I sneaked down the back stairs onto the piazza in search of my own coffee and croissant. In due course the three of them joined me. Over another coffee one of them got out the hotel bill and suggested that we should split it four ways – "After all, padre, you did share our hotel room." Fortunately, and before I could respond, the other two put him very firmly in the picture, and the situation was saved. I was telling this story sometime later and was encouraged not to think too badly of this young officer who is now a member of the House of Lords. One of the Subalterns, Harry Nickerson, quietly suggested that, "If you owned a castle with 95 windows, you too would look after your pennies pretty carefully."

It is Sarajevo however, and not Venice, that has become my favourite city. A mixture of history and beauty and personal experiences blend together to make this a magical place for me.

The name Sarajevo for so many people is immediately linked with the assassination of Archduke Franz Ferdinand of Austria in June 1914, which triggered the start of the first World War. More recently, of course, for some of us is the memory of the Winter Olympics Games of 1984, when Jayne Torvill and Christopher Dean were crowned the Olympic ice-skating champions. More than 24 million people watched the British couple score maximum points at the Zetra Stadium, Sarajevo for their slow, sensuous free dance performance to the music of Ravel's *Bolero*.

The story of the city also includes The Siege of Sarajevo, the longest siege of a capital city in the history of modern warfare which ran from 5 April 1992 to 29 February 1996, and in which a total of 13,952 people were killed, including 5,434 civilians.

There are many reminders of these tragic years around the city, and some of them are found in the pavements around the brewery. The water supply of the brewery drew the population out onto the streets, ducking and diving between the buildings, as they made their way to get their plastic bottles refilled, but thereby exposing themselves to rifle fire from the snipers on the surrounding hills. The names of many of those killed thus are remembered in brass plates in the pavement.

The plaques are often alongside 'Sarajevo roses' – memorials made from scars in the concrete caused by mortar shell explosions. The shells created a unique fragmentation pattern that looks almost floral in arrangement. Later these were filled with red resin, and therefore have been named 'roses'. There are around 200 'roses' in the entire city, and they mark locations where at least three persons were killed during the siege.

These reminders of the Balkan conflict stirred many personal memories for me of watching television news reports from the comfort of home in the UK. The bombing, for example, of the busy marketplace in 1994 when a mortar bomb exploded in the main market of the city centre killing 68 and wounding 150 people. It was the worst single atrocity in Sarajevo during the conflict between Bosnia's Serbs, Muslims and Croats. I also remembered the powerful images of the mortar fire which destroyed the maternity hospital. The shell of that building was still in place, during my time in the city, as a stark reminder of the mindlessness of so much fighting.

Christine and our daughter Caroline were able to fly out to spend a few days with me while I was in Sarajevo. I had become friendly with an ex-RAF corporal who had married a local lass and was now working in the city. His wife, Marsha, offered to give my visitors their own personal battlefield tour of the region. Marsha had been born in Sarajevo and grew up in a happy multi-ethnic community which was almost completely free of any tensions between different nationalities and religions. She told us that her own mother first suspected that things were changing, and for the worse, when Marsha came home from school one day and asked, "Am I Catholic or Orthodox?" The family didn't practise any religion, but in fact her mother was from a Catholic background and so probably with Croatian roots, while her father's family were Orthodox and therefor probably Serbian. The historical three way split between Muslim Bosniacs, Catholic Croats and Orthodox Serbs was starting to rear its head yet again, and life became very ugly in the months and years that followed.

Marsha spent a whole morning and afternoon slowly and carefully sharing her own story and the experiences of her beloved city with Christine and Caroline. They were stunned by the horror of man's inhumanity to man during a siege which took place on mainland Europe, not really that far from home in Scotland, and which had left so much devastation of lives and memories as well as buildings.

Nearly ten years had passed since the signing of the Dayton Agreement in December 1995 but the brokenness of the Balkans in general and BiH in particular was still very far from healed. I was heading up a team of chaplains who were seeking to provide pastoral and moral support to troops who were doing their best to facilitate that healing process. There was not much visible danger or violence, but it was clear that there were many powers pushing their own agenda, often sailing pretty close to the wind when it came to their regard for the law. The civilian population carried their emotional pain openly, broke buildings and broken people struggling to survive in a broken financial syste and broken political climate.

It was a huge privilege to serve as Senior chaplain in that situation. I becam good friends with Slavko Hadzic, the pastor of an independent church based i Sarajevo. When I found myself in Butmir Camp on a Sunday evening I woul often take a few soldiers along with me to Slavko's church service. When returned to Scotland to take up the position of minister of Shawlands Kirk i Glasgow, we adopted Slavko as our missionary partner. Once a year a team fror Shawlands would visit Sarajevo for a week or so, taking gifts from the people c Glasgow, and becoming involved in the evangelical and humanitarian work. helped to maintain and strengthen my love of Sarajevo.

Chapter 14
One Army with a Firm Base

"The human race is not made up of superheroes and heroes but people going about their ordinary business." — Anon

People join the army for all sorts of reasons. I met one soldier who joined the army for a dare. He and his mates were walking down the Sauchiehall Street in Glasgow one sunny afternoon, they passed the army Recruiting officer, and one of them said, "I bet you wouldn't walk in there and sign up." This guy did, joined the Royal Highland Fusiliers and had a very successful career as an infantry soldier. He was a Sergeant when I knew him.

Another soldier told me that his life had been in a serious mess. He was in low-paid insecure employment, he had got his girlfriend pregnant, and he was under pressure from her parents to 'do the decent thing' and get married... but where would they stay? Living with the in-laws didn't sound very attractive. Someone told him that if he joined the army, they would be given their own house, a married quarter, straightaway. Employment, housing, getting away from the in-laws and an escape route from some pretty near scrapes with the police. He was straight down to the recruiting office.

Of course, there are many others who have signed up because of their family traditions of military service, or because they just know that this is the life for them, serving Queen and Country, soldiering at home and overseas, wearing the uniform, learning the skills... perhaps there are almost as many reasons for joining up as there are recruits on every in-take course.

What they all have in common, what all military people have in common, is that they step out of civilian life into a military community which is very different from life as they had experience it so far. It is not quite walking through CS

Lewis's wardrobe into the fictional land of Narnia, but sometimes it can feel like it.

There is a lot in military life which is quite different from civilian life, but there is also, of course, much that is shared by these two parts of our nation. Soldiers start off as civilians, and so bring a lot of their 'baggage', the good stuff along with the bad stuff, into the military community with them. The army reflects civilian society in all sorts of ways.

The relationship between the military and civilian societies has changed dramatically over my 40-year involvement in army chaplaincy. In the late 1970s the general public seemed to show very little interest in service personnel and their welfare. Our nation accepted that we needed the Armed Forces, but there was little interaction between those with military service experience and those without. This was seen in the low numbers of people attending the annual Remembrance Sunday services and parades. While the Festival of Remembrance hosted by The Royal British Legion in the Royal Albert Hall every year was a wonderful spectacle, much of it was entertainment rather than remembrance military bands, marching displays and artillery gun races were the main attraction.

During my years as minister of Shawlands Kirk on the south side of Glasgow from 2005 to 2011, we had developed a very meaningful remembrance season Military operations in Iraq and Afghanistan had raised the profile and importance of remembrance across the nation and I was keen that as a parish church in a prominent position at the centre of our community, we would respond to the opportunity to connect with the public and also to serve them in a meaningful way.

The congregation of Shawlands Kirk worked with Poppy Scotland to become the local organisers for the Poppy Collection, distributing tins and boxes of poppies to over 50 shops and businesses, schools and clubs around the Shawlands area. After remembrance Sunday we would gather these in and count the takings. It was a sizeable task which involved a large team and helped us to feel part of the wider national event. It is amazing how much people enjoy counting money, even when it is not their own. We had to use an elderly lady's shopping basket on wheels to transport the counted cash along the road to the bank.

Shawlands Kirk is fortunate to have a grassed garden which opens right on to the busy junction of Shawlands Cross. Using the model of St Margaret's

Church, Westminster in London, and Princes Street Gardens in Edinburgh, we created a Garden of Remembrance and at 11:00 hours on 11 November each year we held a short Act of Remembrance. This grew over my six years in Shawlands and was attended by pupils from local state and private schools who joined a good number of members of our congregation and the local community. Perhaps the most moving element of these services was listening as a ten-year-old primary school pupil read the Tryst, 'They shall grow not old, as we that are left grow old...' There was seldom a dry eye amongst the older folk in attendance.

The Remembrance Sunday Service also grew in relevance during my time as minister of this parish. The now First Minister of Scotland, Nicola Sturgeon was the local MSP, and she would join us for the service and read the Bible Lesson. I encouraged veterans to wear their medals, and the standards of the local youth organisations were paraded. Our piper on these occasions came from the local Veterans Club and had been a Jock in 1 RHF back in 1977 when I first joined up. He took delight one day in telling our organist, Fiona Hepburn who he felt had tried to boss him about over his piping at a wedding, that he and I had history that went back to 1977. Fiona wasn't at all impressed by our military connections; "Well I was his teacher in Primary five in Killermont School a long time before he joined the army!"

With all of this in place I was faced with a bit of a dilemma in 2008 when Rev Peter Eagles, the assistant chaplain general of 2nd division with its headquarters based at Craigiehall, Edinburgh, phoned up to ask if I would attend the Festival of Remembrance in the Royal Albert Hall on the Saturday evening prior to Remembrance Sunday. This particular year the RBL were marking the Centenary of the Territorial Army. Peter explained that, "The Royal British Legion have requested a serving Church of Scotland TA chaplain with operational experience to receive the Standards, and you are the obvious choice."

"Let me just check a couple of details and I'll get back to you shortly," I responded, playing for time.

For many of us the annual Festival of Remembrance is the highlight of our national season of Remembrance. Taking part in such a wonderful event in the presence of the Queen was something I did not want to turn down, but how on earth could I explain to the good folk of Shawlands that, having built up our own Remembrance event, I was pulling out of the Sunday service and would be in London instead?

I made a couple of phone calls and eventually found someone who explained to me that at the end of the event Her Majesty would leave The Royal Albert Hall by 21:00 hours and, at that stage, I would be free to depart. I worked out that if I hired a car and managed to get away by 22:00 hours, I could be back in Glasgow by about five o'clock in the morning in time for a few hours in bed prior to reporting to church in time for a 10:45 start to our Remembrance Sunday Service.

Having agreed to take part I soon realised firstly that the plan was pretty mad, and secondly that I really had no idea what my involvement in the event really entailed. However, it all ran smoothly. It was a great honour to be involved in the Festival of Remembrance, representing RAChD in general and TA chaplains in particular. It was quite nerve wracking, especially when Bishop Nigel McCulloch, National chaplain to the Royal British Legion, told me off during the rehearsal for saying 'causes of goodness of truth' in my prayer rather than the singular 'cause of goodness of truth' written in the Order of Service. "Remember Her Majesty will be following along and will notice any mistakes." As you can imagine, that did nothing to calm my nerves.

My plan worked out perfectly. Two cans of Red Bull and a couple of Pro Plus caffeine tablets kept me awake on my overnight drive back to Glasgow. (I had never used either before, so it was all a bit of an experiment, which I have not been daft enough to repeat!) I awoke next morning after three hours sleep with pupils the size of saucers, and conducted my service in Shawlands Kirk, attended a curry lunch with the 52nd Lowland troops who had been on parade on George Square, Glasgow, before rushing through to Edinburgh to take the 7th/ 9th Royal Scots Remembrance Service at East Claremont Street TA Centre in Edinburgh.

It was a couple of days before I slept properly again but I was sufficiently recovered for 11 November when we held our now traditional Act of Remembrance in the garden of Shawlands Kirk, and I breathed a sigh of relief, and reflected on the fact that I really did need to learn to say no sometimes.

TA100 was a year-long celebration of the centenary of the Territorial Army, which over its one-hundred-year history has seen almost as many changes and adaptions as the Regular Army. Many of the changes were the result of the UK Government's Regular Defence Reviews.

The passing of The Reserve Forces Act in 1996 resulted in considerable change. This allowed individual Reservists to be compulsorily called up for

ployment and resulted in the TA increasingly being used to provide support
r the Regular Army overseas including, in Bosnia, Kosovo, Cyprus and the
alkland Islands.

In 2003, 9,500 reservists were mobilised to take part in Operation TELIC,
e invasion of Iraq, and over the following ten years or so, approximately 1,200
eservists were deployed annually on tours of duty in Iraq, Operation HERRICK
Afghanistan and elsewhere, normally on six month-long roulements.

In the 2012 Defence Review it was announced that the TA would be renamed
e 'Army Reserve'. The number of regular soldiers would fall from 102,000 to
2,000, and number of reservists would double to 30,000. Reservists would, in
e words of the Defence Secretary, "become an integral part of the army", and
was hoped that a good number of those leaving the slimmed down regular
rces would join the reserves.

Throughout all this time the term 'One Army Concept' was often heard in
onversation. Reservist soldiers really did want to believe that such a thing
xisted, and their belief that parity was on its way was given a huge injection of
onfidence with the change of Conditions of Service in 2015. This guaranteed
rmy Reserve personnel a military Pension based on the number of days they
vere on duty with the reserves, in addition to an extra day's pay for every seven
ays worked in lieu of leave.

I served 24 years as Reservist, and thoroughly enjoyed my time. The bulk of
ny service was as Padre of what is now 52nd Lowland, 6th Battalion the Royal
legiment of Scotland, though in the final few years I became increasingly
nvolved in supporting the senior chaplain in Brigade Headquarters.

The headquarters building in Craigiehall on the north side of Edinburgh
hanged from being Headquarters Scotland (army) to the Headquarters of 2nd
Division in 2007 as part of army restructuring. The assistant chaplain general of
nd Div was now known as the senior chaplain Scotland. This was a full colonel
ank appointment, which was supported by a full-time clerical assistant.

When Army Headquarters Scotland was merged with 51st Infantry Brigade
t Forthside Barracks, Stirling, the senior chaplain changed from being a CF1
full Colonel) to a CF2 (Lt Colonel), and the clerical assistance disappeared
long with the higher rank.

When this change was happening, and prior to the appointment of the first
DACG 51 Brigade, the Brigadier Commander, David Alfrey MBE requested that
he Department appoint a chaplain to work in his headquarters in Stirling. There

was as yet no establishment for a regular chaplain post, and so I was recruited fill the gap as an OCF (Officiating Chaplain to the Forces.) This appointme: was the start of a 12-year history of my involvement in working as part of tl chaplaincy team at the Brigade Headquarters. I was there on my own for a tim and then later I supported both Padre Benjamin Abeledo and Padre Co Maynard when they were DACG, 51 Brigade and HQ Scotland.

I really enjoyed my time in the Brigade Headquarters. It was good to be ab to provide staff chaplain support to my colleagues, and they appreciated m experience and administrative skills. Perhaps it was especially enjoyable when provided cover for them during the times when they were on leave. I never ha any expectation of actually being personally in charge for any length of time, s it was a great surprise when that happened.

Christine and I were lunching at a lovely restaurant in Edinburgh. It was m birthday, but the more important aspect of the day was the recce we were doin of Hotel du Vin as a location for a special party we were planning. It all looke ideal and we were enjoying a pre-lunch drink in the sun-drenched courtyar when the mobile phone in my pocket started to vibrate. Ever the romantic, glanced to see who was calling. It was Cole Maynard my army boss, DACG 51 and HQ Scotland. He had left a message. "It might be important," I suggestec as I wandered off to a quiet corner to listen to what Cole had to say.

Cole's message was that the chaplain general had just phoned him to discus his being deployed to South Sudan on the newly created Operation TRENTON Cole was in his final 18 months of regular service and held the rank of CF2 (L Col). It was very unusual for a chaplain in these circumstances to be mobilisec and so it was quite an unusual request... but one of those military requests fo which there really is only one answer – "Yes, sir!"

The reason he needed to speak to me was because of the suggestion from th CG that I could cover Cole's desk while he was out of the country for six month plus the period preparing to deploy and his post-tour leave.

My response was pretty immediate. What a great opportunity, and what wonderful end to my military career, which had just over a year to run before turned 65. After hearing this news, I had to work hard to concentrate on the rea matters at hand that day, which were celebrating my birthday and enjoying lunch with Christine.

Cole Maynard did deploy as the first chaplain on Op TRENTON, and my si months as stand-in DACG went smoothly. I used the weekly day off from my parish in Duns in the Scottish Borders and spent every Monday in the army office in Stirling. To maximise the time, I would drive up to the officers' mess at Craigiehall, Edinburgh, on a Sunday evening. The Craigiehall Camp Commandant was my old friend and previous KOSB Rugby second-in-command Major John Currie. John had gone out of his way, massaged the mess rules, and arranged a bedroom for me which I could keep throughout the seven months despite the fact that I usually only used it two nights a week. After a good night's sleep and a hearty cooked breakfast served in the wonderful splendour of the mess dining room, I would drive up to Stirling and be at 'my' desk by 08:30 hours.

Knowing that dinner was served at 19:00 hours back in the Mess meant that I could get a clear nine or ten hours' work done, before returning to Edinburgh. I kept Tuesdays flexible so that after another night in the mess, I could either be back in the parish by mid-morning, or out and about doing chaplaincy business. I don't think the parish ever missed me, and I seemed to cover all the requirements of the DACG post.

Although my army reserve commission ran out in July 2018, I have continued to support the present DACG, Rev Duncan Macpherson as Staff Chaplain Scotland. When I turned 65, I was appointed as an OCM (Officiating Chaplain to the Military) and this allows me to support Duncan and where necessary, cover for him. I imagine that I will soldier on in this role for a few more years.

One of the high-profile aspects of the work of the headquarters at 51 Brigade in Stirling was developing and maintaining a strong effective relationship between the army and civilian society. This had become an increasingly important item on the agenda of the Brigade, and involved improving the connection between the Scottish government, the people of Scotland and the military units based in Scotland.

A change of attitude had taken place in society, and there was an increasing awareness in the civilian community that our military personnel weren't somewhere out there in a foreign land fighting a battle on our behalf, but that serving and veteran service men and women, and their dependants were here in the community they had originally come from. They lived here, went to school here, needed housing here, applied for social care here, and used the civilian medical and dental services like everybody else. Soldiers start off life as civilians, and they return to being civilians at the end of their military service.

The repeated sight of Union Flag draped coffins of young servicemen and women being carried off military aircraft at RAF Brize Norton had a powerful impact on all of society, civilian and military, serving and veteran. The operations in Iraq and Afghanistan brought the role of the military home. We started to see ourselves more clearly as one nation, civilian and military. If we really wanted effective Armed Forces who would defend our nation and stand up for peace and justice when we required them to do so, then all of society needed to embrace and support them as part of the whole community.

The 'Firm Base' concept developed with an agenda to deal with issues which related to the overlap between the Armed Forces, the government agencies and the range of service organisations and charities. This was particularly strong in Scotland where it became the practical outworking of the requirements of the military covenant.

The term military covenant came into common use in 2000 to refer to the mutual obligations between our nation and its Armed Forces. It was a way of measuring whether the government and society at large have kept to their obligations to support members of the armed forces and went some way to answering the question of whether adequate safeguards, rewards and compensation were being provided for military personnel who risk their lives in obedience to military orders resulting from the policy of the government. It was argued that armed forces personnel should expect to be treated fairly by the Crown and expect the support of the nation, society and the government.

The Ministry of Defence stated:

In putting the needs of the nation, the army and others before their own, they forgo some of the rights enjoyed by those outside the Armed Forces. So, at the very least, British soldiers should always expect the nation and their commanders to treat them fairly, to value and respect them as individuals, and to sustain and reward them and their families.

Many local authorities and business organisations signed up to the military covenant. While this is to be welcomed, it is not always clear what difference this has brought about apart from a pretty framed certificate on someone's office wall. There needs to be continued pressure brought to bear to ensure that our serving and veteran military personnel and their dependants really do get a fair deal.

I was present in the Great Hall of Edinburgh Castle when the Church of Scotland signed up for the military covenant. There had been considerable debate before the signing was agreed. Much of this surrounded the issue of the UK's nuclear deterrent, and the Kirk's traditional opposition to it. Despite all sorts of wise words and promises, I would have to confess to personally being very sceptical that my own national church has really done very much to keep its side of the covenant. Though I am not at all sure what 'keeping our side of the covenant' would actually entail.

Chapter 15
Closing Reflections

"We want you there as a part of our community, but we are not at all clear who you are, what you are, or what you are supposed to do." —Padre John Vernon

Rev John Vernon included the above quotation when writing the concluding comments to his Mid-Service Clergy Course Research Project in 1983, in which he summed up the overall response shared by the majority of military personnel when asked about the contribution made by army chaplains to service life.

The army does like having chaplains around but isn't quite sure what it is that they do, and that is often not helped by chaplains also often being a little vague themselves. All these years after John's paper the situation is pretty much still the same.

In the summer of 1977, prior to my heading off to Bagshot Park and Sandhurst to start my military career, Christine and I visited her sister-in-law's parents in Dunfermline. Mr Adams had recently retired from a career working in the Royal Navy Dockyard at Rosyth. He had been there as a civilian engineer all his working days and had observed a lot of military life over that time. When he heard that I was about to become an army chaplain, he commented, and not in a negative way, "You'll be a social worker then. That's what chaplains spend most of their time doing."

A social worker? That was certainly not how I imagined myself spending my time. I probably told myself that his evaluation of chaplaincy was based on the Royal Navy, and life for me in the army would be totally different.

About a year later I was sitting in the lecture room at Bagshot Park attending my first Church of Scotland Army Chaplains Annual Conference. Our guest speaker was a World War One chaplain, who shared fascinating reminiscences. He was a skilled orator with a great story to tell. In reply to a question after his talk, I remember him summing up his role on the Western Front, "I was often the 'joker in the pack' providing some levity and relief in the midst of some very dark days." He suggested that all chaplaincy shared this aspect.

A joker in the pack? Again, I found myself questioning the wisdom of an older gentleman. I just couldn't see myself ever filling that role.

And then, more recently, after I had given a lunchtime talk on army chaplaincy, one of the more senior men spoke out during the time for questions. "How would you respond to my old friend who told me that he never had much time for the chaplain? He said that the YMCA and the various welfare organisations were all much better at keeping our morale high during R&R and before we had to return to the front."

No time for the chaplain? I mumbled a response but failed to give a well-reasoned answer to his question, but he did make me think a lot.

I am now very comfortable with all three of these responses to my role and ministry as an army chaplain.

Over many years I realised that it was often in the midst of providing practical social care and counselling for my soldiers and their families that most opportunities arose for me to share something of the love of God and the message of the Christian Gospel. The truth is that practical care and support very often speak more clearly than spoken words, and they often open the door to deep spiritual discussion.

Keeping quiet can be hard, especially for clergy. What is it, they say? "Church of Scotland Ministers don't talk for a long time; it just feels like it." I found that sometimes a jocular word is worth its weight in gold. After a few years of serving as Padre to a variety of infantry units, I had become pretty knowledgeable about tactics and navigation and logistics and all sorts of military skills. There were times when it would have been all too easy, but all so wrong, for me to correct or add to the instructions given out by a young officer to his soldiers.

Humour is often an important safety valve in military life. The stress and tension of life on active service can become overwhelming and introducing some lightness to break through the cloud of heaviness can help everybody. Often it is only the padre who can take the risk of saying something silly, introducing a stupid comment, or making a joke. Just as long as the chaplain doesn't come over as an expert in someone else's field.

The last thing the army wants is a padre who can do someone else's job better than the person in the job itself. Well, actually, perhaps the last thing is a padre who comes onto the rifle range and shoots better than the soldiers. "Come on, Padre, have a go!" is always a welcome cry after a couple of hours watching soldiers shooting. They love to see you getting involved, but really don't want you to get the top score of the day.

I would often 'have a go'. I even managed to achieve 'Marksman' on the sub-machine gun but I think everyone else was a marksman as well that day. My only moment of real success on the ranges was one day at Otterburn in Northumberland with the Scots Guards. We were firing the SA80 rifle at targets 200 yards down the range. I was in the far-right hand lane, and immediately on my left was the commanding officer. Even if I could have, I probably would not have purposely fired some rounds into the CO's target, but that is what I did by mistake. The commanding officer managed one of the best scores in the Battalion that day, and he was, as they say, "chuffed to NAAFI breaks!" His padre smiled quietly despite his own embarrassingly low target score.

And yes, the YMCA staff being more popular than the padres? The YMCA is one of a number of Christian and voluntary organisations that has provided welfare support to the military community. Often this support took the form of recreational facilities in an alcohol-free environment. The Church Army staff, the WRVS ladies and many others provided for the soldiers during their down time and were often the place where soldiers could find a much-needed listening ear.

The popularity of these agencies over the unit padre was partly due to basic fact that a lot of chaplaincy work was conducted during the working day at the place of work. On active service this would be in the midst of the fighting, up at the front, sharing the discomfort of the battle, and dealing with the injured and the survivors in the midst of the killing. The supporting agencies had the equally important, but quite different, task of supporting the troops away from the front. The roles were chalk and cheese, and hard to compare.

As I look back, of all the aspects of army chaplaincy which have changed over these past four decades of my own military service, the most striking to me is the age range of the chaplains themselves. This is probably particularly true among Church of Scotland chaplains. Of the six of us who were commissioned as new chaplains between 1976 and 1979 the average age was 25½. I don't believe there are any chaplains serving at the moment who are under 30 years of age. Like all Christian organisations RAChD is fishing in an ever-decreasing pool of potential chaplains, a pool with fewer and fewer young men and women.

At the other end of the career package the retirement age of chaplains has been increased remarkably. When I was commissioned as a regular the retirement age was 50. When I finally hung up my boots as a reservist, after completing five one-year 'over age extensions' beyond the normal retirement age of 60 years, I was 65. The extensions of service are, of course, largely to compensate for the shortage of new recruits joining the chaplains' department.

During the early stages of setting out to write this book I took advantage of the Church of Scotland Ministers' Study Leave Scheme which allows each parish minister a couple of weeks away from the parish each year to read, research and study. I used some of my allocation to access the library at the Armed Forces Chaplaincy Centre at Amport House, and then spent a reading week at Oxford University funded by the Farmington Institute.

In order to justify the time off from the parish, and the expenses which are paid, participants are required to produce evidence that the study leave was beneficial. I decided that alongside researching for my own writing, I would try and answer the question, "Does a period of military chaplaincy make one a better parish minister?"

The majority of chaplains return to parish ministry after their time in the military. I thought it would be interesting to see how serving and retired chaplains felt about this. Forty-five chaplains responded to my informal survey, fifteen of whom were veterans who either had worked, or still are working, as parish ministers after their army chaplaincy time was over. Every one of them was very much of the opinion that the experience of serving in the army had had a beneficial influence upon their ability to work as civilian clergy. Communication and inter-personal skills were high up on the scale of particular elements which they believed were most powerfully enhanced by military service. Everyone recognised that the limited age range of the military community restricted some aspects of ministry development, but they all agreed that a few years serving in RAChD would enhance any young minister's preparation for a career as a parish minister.

There was a time in the second half of last century when many ex-military chaplains might have found it quite difficult to find a civilian parish at the conclusion of their military service. The profile of the Armed Forces was low, the anti-nuclear movement was very active, and there was a strong correlation between pacifism and much of the more evangelical parts of the church. Chaplains were seen as being in favour of warfare, and many church folks felt that serving in the army was incompatible with true Christianity.

That has all changed considerably and many churches welcome the opportunity of having a minister who can include veterans in the life and work of the church, who is comfortable in addressing military issues, and has the ability to communicate right across society with a simple clarity. Those with experience of ministry in the Armed Forces will almost always have these skills.

I often tell people that the army has been good to me, and it has. Military life suited me in all sorts of ways, perhaps partly because it permitted me to continue being a bit of a rugby playing, party animal at the same time as exercising an effective Christian ministry. But I believe it was more than that.

The late Rev Farquhar Lyall, my first assistant chaplain general, told me in 1977 that the most important thing for an army chaplain was to love the Jocks, and I have never forgotten that. Farquhar knew a lot about soldiers and soldiering. In his Scottish District Notes in the RAChD Journal of December 1980, Rev James Harkness wrote:

Rev J Farquhar Lyall retired as ACG Scotland in April 1980 marking the end of an era for Church of Scotland chaplains. Farquhar was the last of our number who had seen service during the Second World War. Having served as a combatant, he returned to university to complete his studies. After ordination he joined the RAChD and on his retirement had completed almost thirty-one years as a chaplain.

Farquhar had been adjutant of the Black Watch and knew well that soldiers sometimes do the most stupid things. They can behave really badly and can be hugely resistant to the Gospel, but they really are the salt of the earth.

I did not find them hard to love, and when I did struggle God helped me out with some of His love for them, and I think that all in all it helped me to be as good for the army as the army was for me.

Appendix A
My Military Career

My military career spanned over four decades:

August 1977	Commissioned and ordained as a Church of Scotland Army Chaplain.
Attended	RAChD Centre, Bagshot Park and RMA Sandhurst.
October 1977	1st Battalion, Royal Highland Fusiliers, Redford Barracks, Edinburgh.
	Provided cover in Belize.
September 1988	1st Battalion, King's Own Scottish Borderers, Fort George, Inverness.
	Operation BANNER, West Belfast.
	Exercise TRUMPET DANCE, Fort Campbell, Kentucky, USA.
June 1980	Arms plot move with 1 KOSB to Quebec Barracks, Osnabruck.
July 1982	Posted to 1st Battalion Scots Guards, Fort Stanley, Hong Kong.
	2 chaplaincy trips to both Nepal and Brunei.
April 1984	Arms plot move with 1SG to Elizabeth Barracks, Pirbright.
	Exercise PONTE VECCHIO, Italy.
	Operation BANNER, Bessbrook Mill, South Armagh.
March 1987	Posted to 1st Battalion Black Watch, Montgomery Barracks, Berlin.

June 1989	Posted to 1st Battalion Royal Scots, Werl, West Germany.
	Operation GRANBY, The First Gulf War.
August 1981	Arms plot move with 1RS to Fort George, Inverness.
	Operation BANNER, Bessbrook Mill, South Armagh.
August 1993	PVR (Premature Voluntary Retirement).
August 1995	Granted a Type A TA Commission.
August 1995	Attached to 32 Signal Regiment (Volunteers).
	Senior chaplain during Foot and Mouth emergency 2001.
December 2001	Posted to 52nd Lowland Regiment.
March 2005	Appointed senior chaplain UK NSC Banja Luka, and EUFOR.
January 2017	Appointed acting DACG 51 Infantry Brigade and HQ Scotland.
July 2018	Retired from army Reserve on reaching 65 years of age.
October 2018	Appointed as Officiating Chaplain to the Military in the role of Staff Chaplain Scotland.

Appendix B
My Commanding Officers

served with 19 commanding officers during my four decades of service within
e RAChD:

REGULAR SERVICE
Brig John Drummond CBE ADC RHF
Brig Colin Mattingley CBE KOSB
Maj Gen Tim Toyne-Sewell KOSB
Brig Iain McLaughlin OBE SG
Brig Kim Ross OBE SG
Lt Gen Sir John Kiszely KCB MC SG
Lieutenant General Sir Alistair Irwin, KCB, CBE
Brig Donald Wilson CBE BW
Col Martin Gibson OBE RS
Brig Iain Johnstone OBE
Lt Col Bill Sylvester BA RS

RESERVE SERVICE
Col Alan Lapsley TD RSigs
Lt Col Jim McKee RSigs
Lt Col Ian Pickard BA RHF
Col Jim Wilson KOSB
Brig Charles Coull SCOTS
Lt Col Charles Platt SCOTS
Col Gary Stimson SCOTS
Lt Col Jules McIlveney SCOTS

Appendix C

Employment of UK Army Chaplains
During the First Gulf War

During the build-up to Op GRANBY which is now more often referred to as the First Gulf War, there was much discussion regarding how the Christian ministers serving as military chaplains in the coalition forces would operate in Saudi Arabia with its strict Islamic laws. The US military had taken a particular stance and so there was a requirement to define with some clarity what UK army chaplains would and would not do. Rev James Harkness had strong views, and these were summarised in the following Joint Headquarters paper:

ANNEX I to JHQ/2/PLANS Dated 14 Jan. '91

EMPLOYMENT OF PADRES

1. The following guidelines apply to the employment of chaplains in Saudi Arabia.

a. Spiritual care for all UK military personnel should be readily available.

b. Clerical equipment should be kept out of sight in transit between unit locations.

c. Small black crosses may be worn on shirt collars, except when there is a risk of causing local offence (e.g., when travelling on public roads). Clerical collars are not to be worn. There are no restrictions on head-dress or cap badges.

d. In the event of hostilities, a white armlet bearing a red cross is to be worn in accordance with Article 40 of the First Geneva Convention 1949.

e. Chaplains should use their discretion as to where worship should be conducted. In general, it is preferable for services to be held indoors. Where no suitable covered accommodation is available services may be conducted outdoors provided no local nationals are present or in the vicinity. Several smaller services are preferable to one large service. Any documents / leaflets prepared for services are to be collected after the service. No public announcements should be made where local nationals can hear or see them.

f. Attendance at services should be restricted to military personnel and civilian UK national support staff.

g. Chaplains should carry their standard military ID card (modified for RAF chaplains to remove mention of clerical role) and F Ident 107 at all times.

h. Chaplains should have no contact with the media. Press lines to be used by military spokesmen are as follows:

Q. Are there / will there be chaplains deployed to Saudi Arabia?

A. Arrangements are always made for the pastoral and spiritual support of UK forces, taking into account of the circumstances of their deployment. Not prepared to comment on the precise arrangements in the Gulf.

Q. Are there / have the Saudis agreed guidelines of chaplains in Saudi Arabia?

A. No comment.

Q. Are we following the US example in deploying chaplains?

A. US arrangements are a matter for the US.

Appendix D
ORBAT

1st Battalion the Royal Scots (The Royal Regiment)
Order of Battle, Op GRANBY Dec 1990 – April 1991

BATTLE GROUP HEADQUARTERS

Commanding Office	Lt Col Iain Johnstone OBE
Second in Command	Major Kirk Gillies MBE
Adjutant	Capt George Lowder
RSM WO1	Rab Fraser
Operations Officer	Capt Neil Brownlie
Operations WO	WO2 Brown
Intelligence Officer	Capt Dermont Fulton
Intelligence NCO	CSgt Lusty
Signals Officer	Capt Jim Springthorpe
Training Officer	Capt Steve Telfer
Watchkeeper	2 Lt Allsopp Grenadier Guards
	Pipe Major Cornwall
Liaisons Officer	Lt Alex Dockar 2Lt Stewart Henderson

A COMPANY

Officer Commanding	Maj Norman Soutar MC
Second in Command	Capt Bob Bruce
2nd Captain	Lt Chris Brannigan
CSM	WO2 Flood
CQMS	CSgt Bain
Platoon Commander	Lt Kenny Douglas
Platoon Commander	2Lt Henry Angus

Platoon Commander | Lt Colin Dougan

B COMPANY

Officer Commanding	Maj John Potter RHF MC
Second in Command	Capt Alex Alderson
2nd Captain	Capt Tom Watters
CSM	WO2 Lumsden
CQMS	CSgt Mercer
Platoon Commander	Lt Rob Dickson
Platoon Commander	Lt Alastair Stobie
Platoon Commander	2 Lt Roger Walker

FIRE SUPPORT COMPANY

Officer Commanding	Maj Brian Johnston KOSB
	Capt James Stephenson
Second in Command	Capt J Gillespie-Payne
CSM	WO2 Dickson
CQMS	CSgt Johnstone
Mortar Pl Commander	Capt A Burnett
Mortar Pl 2IC	WO1 Gallagher
Recce Pl Commander	Capt A McLeod
Recce Pl 2IC	CSgt Speirs
Anti-tank Pl Commander	Lt Guy Richardson
Anti-tank Pl 2IC	CSgt Butler
Mobile Main Section	Comd Lt Dicky Donovan

REGIMENTAL AID POST

Regimental Medical Officer	Maj Ronnie Bissett RAMC
Regimental Medical Officer	Capt John Timothy RAMC
Padre Rev Stephen Blakey	RAChD
Ambulance Master	Capt Paul Mehrlich DERR
Bandmaster	WO1 Hodgetts

A2 ECHELON

Officer Commanding	Capt Bill McGrath
Second in Command	Lt Wendy Smart WRAC

Quartermaster (Tech)	Maj Paddy Waugh
RQMS	WO2 McConnell
CQMS	CSgt Skirving / Sgt Finlay
CSM	WO2 Cochrane
Master Chef	WO2 Evans ACC
EME	Capt M Court REME
ASM	WO1 Knighton REME
AQMS	WO2 Bradlet ACC
QMSI	Sgt Young APTC

A1 ECHELON

Motor Transport Officer	Capt David Beveridge
RQMS(T)	WO2 Henderson
MTWO	WO2 Gilmour

B1 ECHELEON

Quartermaster	Maj John Sands
Paymaster	Capt Tony Restall

B2 ECHELON

Assistant Adjutant	Lt Bill Sutherland
Chief Clerk	WO2 Livingstone

REAR PARTY

Officer Commanding	Maj Alan Blamire
Unit Families' Officer	Capt Mick Low MBE

Appendix E

Operation Granby Chaplains

List prepared by The Museum of Army Chaplaincy

1. Rev Basil Pratt	Force Chaplains
2. Rev Alastair Heagerty	Divisional Chaplain and Field Hospital
4. Rev Alun Price	Senior Chaplain, 7 Brigade
5. Rev John Blair	Senior Chaplain, 4 Brigade
6. Rev John Tee	1 Staffords
7. Rev Philip Majcher (CS)	SCOTS GDs
8. Rev Roger Burt	40 Field Regt, RA
9. Rev Christopher Broddle	21 Engineer Regt, RE
10. Rev Kenneth Pillar	10 Regt, RCT
11. Rev Sean Scanlon (RC)	Queen's Royal Irish Hussars
12. Rev David Kelly (RC)	1ST Armoured Division Field Ambulance
13. Rev Adrian Pollard	3 Royal Regiments of Fusiliers
14. Rev Stephen Blakey (CS)	1 Royal Scots
15. Rev David Peachell	$16^{TH}/5^{TH}$ Queen's Royal Lancers
16. Rev Stephen Griffith	26 Field Regiment, RA
17. Rev David Coulter (CS)	2 Field Regiment, RA
18. Rev Geoffrey Sussex (UB)	33 General Hospital, RAMC
19. Rev Alan Finchley (RC)	33 General Hospital, RAMC
20. Rev Stephen Parselle	32 General Hospital, RAMC
21. Rev John Payne	32 Field Hospital, RAMC
22. Rev Kevin Savage (M)	32 Field Hospital, RAMC
23. Rev Andrew Burt	22 Field Hospital, RAMC
24. Rev J Christopher Cook	Divisional Admin Area
25. Rev Kenneth Roach	205 General Hospital, RAMC (V)

26. Rev Iain Barclay   205 General Hospital, RAMC (V)
27. Rev James Duddy (RC)   205 General Hospital, RAMC (V)
28. Rev Michael Scouler (CS) POW DUTY
29. Rev James McLean (CS)   POW DUTY
30. Rev Graham Hadfield
31. Rev Michael Spencer
32. Rev Michael Weymes (RC) 14TH / 20TH HUSSARS

Appendix F
EUFOR in 2005

ational military contributions to EUFOR during my time as senior chaplain:

In theatre troops of the 22 EU nations:

ustria	202
elgium	58
zech Republic	89
stonia	2
inland	183
rance	402
ermany	1180
reece	181
ungary	122
eland	52
aly	1004
atvia	3
ithuania	1
uxemburg	1
etherlands	430
oland	226
ortugal	231
lovakia	4
lovenia	153
pain	467
weden	80
nited Kingdom	727

EU troops 5,798

In theatre troops of the 11 non-EU nations:

Albania	71
Argentina	2
Bulgaria	36
Canada	85
Chile	20
Morocco	133
Norway	17
New Zealand	14
Romania	110
Switzerland	25
Turkey	345

Non-EU troops 858
Total number of troops serving in EUFOR: 6,656 (August 2005)

Appendix G
My Chaplains General

have served with nine Chaplains General between 1977 and 2018:

977–1980	Peter Mallet (Appointed CG in July 1974)
980–1986	Frank Johnston
987–1995	James Harkness
995–2000	Victor Dobbin
000–2004	John Blackburn
004–2008	David Wilkes
008–2011	Stephen Robbins
011–2014	Jonathan Woodhouse
014–2018	David Coulter
018–	Clinton Langston

CPSIA information can be obtained
at www.ICGtesting.com
Printed in the USA
LVHW080500110821
695018LV00001B/1